the 14-day
REBOOT

The Jump-Start You Need to
Lose Weight, Rebalance Hormones
and Detox Your Body

Go online to get your Free Resources
the14dayrebootbook.com

Ordering Information: Quantity sales. Special discounts are available on quantity purchases by corporations, associations, and others. For details, contact the publisher at the address above. Orders by U.S. trade bookstores and wholesalers.
Please contact: 800-273-1625 | support@trevorcrane.com | EpicAuthor.com
First Edition

EPIC AUTHOR
P U B L I S H I N G

For more information about Dr. Raul Serrano or to book him for your next event or media interview, please contact him via email at: Info@DrSerrano.me

Healthcare Disclaimer: The information, including but not limited to, text, graphics, images and other material contained in this book are for informational purposes only. The purpose of this book is to promote broad consumer understanding and knowledge of various health topics. It is not intended to be a substitute for professional medical advice, diagnosis or treatment. Always seek the advice of your physician or other qualified healthcare provider with any questions you may have regarding a medical condition or treatment and before undertaking a new health care regimen, and never disregard professional medical advice or delay in seeking it because of something you have read in this book.

TABLE OF CONTENTS

TOC

SECTION ONE:
IT'S NOT WHAT YOU KNOW, IT'S THE WHY

SECTION TWO:
FOUR STEP REMOVE/REBUILD PROCESS

SECTION THREE:
PUTTING IT ALL TOGETHER AND MAKING IT WORK

DEDICATION

To my "A Team", Adriana, Aria, Atlas and Asa, I love you guys. You are my anchor. I pray the principles in this book have a generational impact on your lives. I can't wait to see how God uses you to impact the world.

To my wife Jessica, I love you. I don't understand how I ended up with such an amazing and Godly woman. You are a true gift from above.

To Jesus, thank You for saving me.

ACKNOWLEDGMENTS

Wow, what a journey. One page for acknowledgments seems so insignificant compared to the amount of work, dedication, help, passion and love so many have poured into this book.

Jodi, thank you for all you have done to put this book together. You are the conductor of an orchestra with out of tune instruments. You made music out of the madness.

Heather, thank you for listening to all my crazy ideas and being so willing to go with the flow. I appreciate all your grace in the process, but most importantly, for being an advocate and encourager.

Brian, you are the like the great and powerful Oz working behind the curtain. Thanks for getting it done and bringing this thing alive online.

Trevor, without your push to make me put a date down, this book would have stayed in my head and never become a reality. Thanks for your accountability and invaluable guidance.

Karen, I can't thank you enough for putting up with my Puerto Rican English through the editing process (that must have been painful).

Max Living, there have been so many Chiropractors in this organization who have mentored me, inspired me and journeyed with me through my career. Thank you to all of the ML family for your passion to change health care and for your heart for humanity. ML, we are just getting started!

Jesus said, "But many who are first will be last, and the last first." To my team, I saved this thank you for the end because I believe you embody what it means to serve others and each other. Thank you so much for everything you have done. There is absolutely no way this book gets done without your encouragement, your love and your hard work in taking things off my plate. It allowed me to have the bandwidth and time to make this book a reality. Laura, Gigi, Deandra, Sheridan THANK YOU! I love you all and I am absolutely thrilled to be on this journey with each one of you!

YOU WERE BORN TO RE-BOOT

Dr. Ben Lerner, *2 X NY Times Best-Selling Author and Founder of Velocity Consulting & Coaching*

Your body is looking to bless you, but also holds you accountable. A remarkable fact about the human body is that even small changes in your lifestyle can create big payoffs in terms of physical, physiological, and immunological changes. Your body has a remarkable ability to begin to reap positive changes the moment you commit to any sort of lifestyle or care that works to its favor. This really takes away the time and effort excuse as it really doesn't require a whole lot of either to begin reaping rewards.

Even better news is that if you're looking for big changes to your health, fitness, and appearance or in fact, a complete reboot, it isn't too hard or painful either. You'll just need slightly more intensity and the kind of direction Dr. Serrano shares here.

If you feel limited at all by your past, your genetics, or that you feel you've just tried it all and all is lost, much can be done to change your future. You do not have to take my word for it as science continues to show us that we can get past our past and DNA is not destiny.

FOREWORD

Two large-scale clinical studies from Northwestern Medicine actually confirmed that important facets of life have far more to do with lifestyle than genetics. A leader in the study and chair and professor of preventive medicine at Northwestern University Feinberg School of Medicine and a staff cardiologist at Northwestern Memorial Hospital Donald Lloyd-Jones, M.D said "Health behaviors can trump a lot of your genetics. This research shows people have control over their health." The actual studies showed that someone who has genes that do not support heart health can improve the state of the heart through a proper lifestyle. Changes to your body and genetics come predictably as long as you address several lifestyle factors at once. The study of 2000 participants referenced here showed that healthy lifestyle choices such as an improved diet, smoking, exercising regularly, and not consuming alcohol excessively dramatically lowered the risk of developing heart disease.

The result of this prestigious study emphasized how important it was to address all of the key areas of lifestyle and not just one or two. The risk of disease only decreased by 6% for participants who changed just one lifestyle factor such as nutrition, while it decreased by 60% (10 times more) for those who made changes to all of the lifestyle factors that were studied.

Daniel David Palmer, the founder of chiropractic, described the human body as a dynamic self-regulating organism that continually seeks to restore and sustain a state of balance and harmony among all of the systems in the body. To Dr. Palmer's point, when we suffer from an injury or develop an infection, the body automatically begins to rebalance or "re-boot." It instantly goes to work, attempting to repair itself or attack the infection. Similarly, we begin to sweat when we are too warm, and we start to shiver when we are too cold. This is the body's way of continuously maintaining a healthy temperature of about 98.6 degrees Fahrenheit (37 degrees Celsius). The same law is in place regarding your outer appearance, fitness levels, and day to day well-being. Your body is actually looking to be restored. Every cell in your system, right now, wants desperately to transform. Every muscle and fiber of your being is seeking its best shape and level of conditioning. All you have to do is hit the button. With the right program and even modest levels of commitment, your body is ready, willing, and able to re-boot.

Your new body is important. It is the vehicle God will use to carry out His great purposes. You matter to the people around you and the people you love, you matter to your assignment, you matter to God, and you matter to history. The rest is up to you.

I have known Dr. Serrano for many years and have seen the results he

FOREWORD

has gotten with his patients and the members of his community. He has put together a proven formula to re-boot your life that is truly transformative. All you have to do is participate in all or even just part of this plan and the whole world starts to change.

- Dr. Ben Lerner

It's Not What You Do; It's Why You Do It

In this section, I get personal. I share my story, my heart and my passion behind all I do. This is the foundation for the entire 14-Day Reboot. My hope is that my story empowers you to connect with your reason for making a change. I also provide simple and effective tools for building a mental starting point so you can be strong and committed to a new lifestyle and a new you.

In this Section:

Chapter One - The Tie, The Door, The ....

Chapter Two - Anchor

Chapter Three - Why 14 Days?

Health Quiz

REAL HEALTH "CARE" TREATS THE CAUSE, NOT THE SYMPTOMS.

The Tie, The Door, The ...

My Heart. My Story.

Growing up I was constantly sick, constantly medicated and constantly in and out of the hospital. I remember it like it was yesterday: the smell of sterile hospital rooms, the white walls, the IV drips and the fear of not knowing what was going to happen next.

I lived in the uncertainty of what was happening with my body, many times being awakened from a deep sleep in the middle of the night for blood draws, more testing or to take more meds. The answer to my health issues was always changing. It all began with bilateral hernia surgery when I was two weeks old followed by antibiotics which, later I came to understand, destroyed my gut health. I spent the better part of elementary school as one of the skinniest kids anyone would ever meet. I was hospitalized so frequently with diarrhea and dehydration the staff coined me, "Mr. Diarrhea." Yeah, it's never good when hospital staff have a nickname for their patients.

Fast forward a few years. I was heading into middle school when the next diagnosis was given to me--hypoglycemia. Hypoglycemia results when your blood sugar drops; and if it drops suddenly, you can pass out. My parents were told I could die or have severe damage to my brain if this happened too frequently. The solution? The doctors told my parents that I needed to keep candy bars and juices readily available "just in case." As you might imagine, giving a middle school boy candy bars and juice instantly initiated a lot of "just in case" moments. My favorite was the king-size Reese's Peanut Butter Cups, that would fit only in the large compartment of my back pack. I feasted on them so often that even now I still have the urge to buy a pack every time I check out at our local grocery store.

In just a few short years, however, "just in case" drove me from being the skinniest kid in my middle school class to being the most obese one. You can imagine the mental, physical, and emotional stress this put on me as a kid. You may remember as I do, the middle school years are filled with raging hormones, new transitions in life, bullying, and trying to figure out who you are. Every time I share my story I am reminded of the summer of 6th grade when my mom bought a blue inflatable whale for our pool. The next day the neighborhood kids questioned me about my twin brother floating around our pool. The morning bus stop always provided a fat joke or another poke at the belly as well. My given nickname was, "Ragu - Old Thick and Chunky Style." I remember often crying myself to sleep, thinking, "Why me?" I was overweight, depressed and my health was beginning to affect every part of my life.

Raul (Middle School)

One weekend I was sitting in my room, and I began to think, "What does the future look like for me?" I loved sports, but could barely keep up with everyone. I thought about my grandparents and how they were overweight and heavily medicated. My mom was always suffering from pain syndromes and other ailments. The doctors led me to believe this was my lot in life, this was

Chapter One

all in my genes, I had no choice and no hope. I believed the lie. I could see my future playing out before me, and it was not how I imagined my life would go.

There was a single moment that changed everything for me.

The memory is vivid. I can visualize my room, what I was wearing, the color of the walls, my bed. I remember feeling hopeless, isolated, with no way to fix my situation. Being fat didn't mean I just wanted to sit around and play video games all day. I still wanted to play sports--and be good at them--but continually being picked last or not at all was deflating. Feeling trapped with no way out, not wanting to live like this for one more day, I walked over to my drawer, opened it and pulled out a tie. I put it around my neck. The other end was knotted and hung over the door, which I shoved closed. The door shut, and I heard the door knob click; it was the last sound I would ever hear. I stepped onto my small stool, tightened the tie around my neck and jumped... SNAP the tie broke. I quickly felt the pain of falling flat on my rear end, and I immediately began to sob, pleading to God, pleading for guidance, pleading for help. I begged God for a way out and all I could say was, "Why, why, why me?"

For years I kept my story private, and it's been only over the past few years I have begun to share my past. It was when I sold my first practice and opened up at my new location that something shifted in me. I don't know what or why, but something told me I needed to unzip, show people my heart and share my story. The reason I share it now is because no child or adult should ever be left hopeless and feeling there is nowhere to turn when it comes to their health. My story is the heart and passion behind this book. God has taken me on an amazing journey to discover what health is, where it comes from and what it means to be truly healthy. Yes, while the focus of this book is nutrition, that is just one aspect of the health puzzle. It is one of the most misunderstood and most confusing aspects of health. For most people trying to regain or maintain their health, nutrition is like being in the middle of a major city you don't know...with no GPS, no maps and no guidance. There are a lot of streets and a lot of options; but which way do you go, what turn do you take, or what road do you travel to arrive at your destination?

Why?... Because...

Why should you do this? Why should you make the change? Because today many people are being told their current conditions or situations are how their lives will go, and there is nothing they can do to change it. Too many

Chapter One

people are falling into a "health care" system that says, "Take this medication to ease your symptoms," yet the system doesn't actually search for the root cause of their ailments. Real health "care" treats the cause, not the symptoms. Yet, people are left thinking disease runs in their families and in their genes; and they are destined to live on medications and make the most of it. This is a lie! I once bought into this. This is why I am passionate about what I get to do...Sharing with people the truth about health and healing.

Today, more than ever, families are pleading for guidance and for help. In this book my team and I give you the knowledge, the answers, and the plans to help navigate the confusing nutritional landscape we are in. This book can change your life. Over the next few months your health status can look drastically different, but it's up to you to act. I encourage you not to wait. Start today. We have made it easy for you to begin your journey to health and healing right now. You don't need to have it all figured out to begin; we have included two sections at the end of each chapter to help you take action. Each chapter includes a summary and a "your turn" section. In these you will find the main points from the chapters and guiding questions to help you take small steps to act on what you have just learned. Are you ready to shed the feelings of being trapped, sick and hopeless? Are you ready to move toward success in your personal life, career and health? Are you ready to experience what your life would look like if your physical and mental health were working at their optimal potential?

Starting and implementing these small steps will begin the process of your building health and not just fighting disease. If you continue to just fight disease, you are simply covering up symptoms; and you aren't moving forward. At best you are getting by, but you'll never thrive. When you cover up symptoms you begin to accept a version of what God intended for all of us. The truth is that God did not create your body broken, you are not a genetic mistake nor are you an overlooked creation. God created your body perfect in His eyes. He created you to be healthy and vibrant, and He gifted you a body with an amazing power to heal itself. Think about it; if you nicked yourself shaving this morning, what did you have to do for the nick to heal? Nothing. Your body would immediately begin to create a small scab to seal and repair the area. In a few hours or days you wouldn't even be able to tell that anything happened.

Why can your body heal a nick or a cut on your skin; but internally it is not healing your hormone problems, heart disease, sugar imbalances, headaches, fibromyalgia, nor weight gain? No, the answer is not genetics. The answer is interference--something is interfering with the healing process. Going back to the nick example, if I gave someone an anti-coagulant (a medication

Chapter One

that prevents clotting in the body), would the body be able to heal the cut at the same rate? No, and, in some cases it would prevent it from healing at all. This is not because the body has lost the ability to heal; it is because something has now interfered with the healing process. This is the same thing that happens internally.

The motto in our home and in our office is:

"God needs no help to heal; He just needs no interference."

Interference in our culture comes from many sources; the key to healing your body and living to your full potential is to find and eliminate the culprits. Toxic foods, pesticides, artificial ingredients, processed foods and many others are all major causes which interfere and decrease your body's ability to heal. All of those things that God did not create are the very same substances that are hurting your body. We will take a deeper dive and walk you through each one of these in this book, but first we need to look at the most important step in this whole process.

At the end of each chapter in sections one and two, a chapter summary and prompt are offered to highlight important information:

Summary

This section will highlight key points from the chapter as refreshers.

Your Turn

This segment will have questions to prompt you to begin assimilating and taking action on the material. These are great questions to discuss with others.

Chapter One

FINDING YOUR

ANCHOR

IS THE MOST

IMPORTANT

STEP OF YOUR

REBOOT.

Anchor

Ruth

It was my second year in practice, and I walked into the exam room to meet my new patient, Ruth. Ruth's first visit involved completing new patient paperwork, a consultation and exam. As I review a patient's paperwork, I stop at one specific section titled, "Goals and Aspirations." In our office this is the most important section because we need to know the reason the patients are there and what they are striving to accomplish; our goal is to come alongside them and help them be healthy enough to achieve these goals. As soon as I got to that section of Ruth's paperwork and asked her why she was there, she began to share, tears filling her eyes. "I always had a vision of retiring and being able to use my time to take mission trips abroad and serve the undeserved. My whole life, that is all I have wanted to do; and now here I am sitting in front of you, retired and with a body that is hurting and broken down. I've already battled cancer, I am overweight, I am on a list of medications that grows bigger every year; and now my doctors tell me I have congestive heart failure, diabetes and am unfit to travel. I am 62, have saved for years waiting for this time in my life to go serve abroad, and now I can't even go."

This is one of many similar stories I have heard through the years. Many of us continue to live life, paying no attention to our health...until the bottom falls out. Then we are left with little hope of ever fully regaining it. I share Ruth's story because, on that day, I began to realize that our health is the most important asset we have. Everything we are meant to accomplish on this Earth depends on it. Our purpose—our calling—is our anchor. It doesn't matter how much money we have, what possessions we own or what visions God puts on our hearts; none of it matters if we lose our health. If we want to regain and keep our health it will take work and a commitment to change; and for this work, for this commitment, to stick we need an anchor.

Find It

Finding your anchor is the most important step of your "Reboot." Whether it's working with athletes, families, or even other health professionals, everyone who has long-term success has an anchor. Your anchor is your reason "why." Your anchor is not why you "should" make the change; it's why you "need" to make the change. Your anchor will motivate you, it will keep you on track, and it will keep you moving forward.

If you are on a boat, the bigger the anchor, the more it will hold. Your health anchor works the same way--the bigger your anchor the more pull it will have, and the more it will help you from drifting. To find a bigger anchor you will need to dig and find something beyond you, something bigger than you and weightier than any excuse that might pull you away from your goal. Let me explain. Suppose someone tells me his reason (anchor) for beginning our program is because he wants to lose a few pounds to look better in a bathing suit for beach season. Yes, that is an anchor; but because it is all about him, it is a very small anchor. This small anchor might hold him in place initially, but as the winds of life begin to blow--vacations or time off, emotional stress, a busy work schedule, family commitments, or the Reese's peanut butter cup at the checkout (Yes, I have an issue with Reese's)--the small anchor of weight loss for summer will not be able to keep him from drifting away from his plan. A bigger anchor would be, "I want to start this program because I have grandkids; and I want to be healthy enough to play and dance with my grandkids." This is a much bigger anchor because you are not only thinking about yourself and something within your future that is in arm's reach, but you are thinking about all that is to come and a place in your future that you can't yet fully see.

There is more weight to this anchor; it affects the next generations in your family, how long and how well you will live. This anchor can shift your whole perspective. This anchor will keep you steady even when the waves come and the winds of life try to pull you away. Anchors are not about looking good in a dress for the big event, or about fitting into your old jeans. It's about thriving well into your 70s, 80s and 90s so that you can reach and fulfill your God-given potential.

So, what is your anchor? Why do you want to make a change? Why do you want to start "The 14-Day Reboot" and the Reboot Lifestyle? Is it for your children or your children's children? Is it for what you want your life to look like in the future? Is it so you can travel and enjoy your later years with your spouse? Is it so you don't end up in a nursing home? What are your goals? What desires has God put in your heart? Take some time before you move on to the next chapter and really begin to think and pray about your ANCHOR. (At the end of this chapter we have given you some questions and prompts to help you find and lock in your anchor.)

No Skipping

Early in my career I was feeling stuck. I was recently married, we had our first baby on the way; and my career was stagnant. We were financially

Chapter Two

stretched thin with student loans and other expenses that come with starting our lives together and preparing for our baby. At work I was struggling. I was not seeing many patients, and I felt like I was working hard but not seeing any progress. I had a call with my mentor, with whom I talked once a week. In this particular conversation he asked me about my morning routine. He asked, "Are you doing the things in the morning to get you ready for your day?" To me this looked like working out, getting in God's Word, and mentally preparing myself. And I said "No." I was off and on, and I gave him a list of excuses why I wasn't consistent. And then he made this statement that changed me from that moment on. He said, "How you do anything, is how you do everything." If I skip out of my routine it will show up in other areas of my life. As life gets crazier and more hectic, bad habits and skipping steps will reveal themselves. Think about this scenario: You are at the gym and you have told yourself you would do 12 reps; you get to that last rep but then you stop at 11. That will carry over into other areas of your life. If I cut corners in my workouts or in my work, where else am I willing to cut corners? Is it with my family, with my finances or, worse, in my spiritual life? Skipping steps, even simple steps, can set you up for patterns or behaviors that can become detrimental to the results you are looking for. And this goes beyond your health. If you take care of the simple things, the more complicated things will take care of themselves.

Anchor

In my 10+ years of practice, the patients who have been able to start and maintain long-lasting changes are the patients who take this first step seriously. I believe there are many reasons why this is true, but here is my number one reason:

When things get tough
will you have the rope to set your anchor?

What will keep you on track and making progress? How will you choose the healthier options when you find yourself at the drive-thru with no one to keep you accountable?

True story. My nutritional journey has not been an easy one because of my early years of fast foods, candy bars and juices. I still struggle with making the best choices. Even with all the nutritional knowledge I have acquired through the years, it all comes down to the moment of decision. If you were to put a coal-fired, pepperoni pizza and a salad in front of me, it would be very difficult for me to choose the salad. But over the years my choices have continued to improve; and it's mainly because I have a solid rope to set my anchor. (Later in the book you will learn about vacation meals, which allow you to have your pizza and still see results!)

Chapter Two

The motto in our home is progress over perfection. A few months after marrying my awesome and beautiful wife, Jess, I went through a season of not making the healthiest choices nutritionally (and I teach this stuff). At the time we had one daughter, and we were over the moon with our growing family. Externally, everything seemed great--a healthy baby, amazing wife, our practice was beginning to grow; but internally I was struggling, and I couldn't figure out why I could not stay on track with my nutritional choices. During this time I was invited to a health conference. At this conference I learned about your "Big Why" (anchor) and the importance of having a reason for change. After leaving that event I crafted my first anchor:

> "To be a leader for my family and create healthy habits so that we can fulfill God's purpose for our lives."

Our instructions were simple; write our anchor on paper, tape it to the bathroom mirror and review it daily for the next 30 days. This is how you add rope to the end of the anchor; this is how you get your anchor to go from your head to your heart. If you are boating and you drop your anchor overboard, it is no good unless you have a rope tied to the anchor to hold the boat in place. With no anchor, you would drift away; and before you know it, you would be far from where you started or where you wanted to be. The same thing happens inside of you. If your anchor stays in your head or written down on paper and never reviewed, it will never get to your heart. When it gets in your heart is when your anchor is set and when change happens. Having your anchor in your heart is how you can make sure that, regardless of the difficulties which come your way, you are able to stay strong and continue to make progress toward your health.

As I read my anchor daily it began to get into my heart. Toward the end of the 30 days I was having a very busy day. I had seen patients all morning, I had a lunch talk at a local business; and I was heading back for my afternoon shift to see another full shift of patients. In all this running around, I found myself starving; and without hesitation I pulled into the Chick-Fil-A drive-thru, because it's the "healthier" fast food. (FYI- I absolutely love the deluxe spicy chicken sandwich they offer.) As I waited in the drive-thru line, however, I began thinking about my anchor; and my internal dialogue began. It went something like, "If my daughter were old enough to understand what was going on and sitting in the back seat, would this be the example I would want to set for her as her leader. Would my ordering the spicy chicken sandwich be creating the healthy habits and examples I would want to pass down to her for her future?" And at the moment of decision, I pulled up to the speaker and

Chapter Two

ordered the garden salad with grilled chicken and on my way I went. At that moment my anchor drove me to make the better decision, not only for me but for those around me who will be impacted by the decisions I make. My choices have been better since then—not always perfect, but better—and that is progress.

Back to Ruth, if you fast forward three months after her initial visit, Ruth had committed to our program. She started by anchoring to the vision God had put in her heart to serve abroad and reading her anchor daily. Ruth was diligent and driven, and she persevered through many tough choices. In three months, she lost 27 lbs., decreased many of her medications by half and was able to get off a few of them completely. Almost exactly one year after the day she walked into our office, she was on a plane taking her first mission trip to Haiti. This was progress.

> My plea to you is do not skip this first step;
> begin now to create and set your anchor.

Begin

Step 1 – Take some time to get away from the noise and be alone.

Step 2 – When you are alone begin by asking God and searching internally what you really want and/or what does He want. Think big, think long term, think about others. Begin to journal and write down your thoughts.

Step 3 – Begin crafting your anchor; as you craft your anchor, know that it can and will change as you go through the process.

Examples:

- To be healthy, because I see myself serving others the rest of my life. Being healthy allows me to live life to the fullest and embrace God's purpose for my life.

- I want to be an example of health for my family.

- I will be the old man dancing at my great-grandkids' weddings.

- To live independently and contribute to those around me for as long as I live.

Step 4 – Write your anchor on a note card and post it where you will see it daily, so you can read and review it throughout your 14-Day Reboot and beyond. (The bathroom mirror is a great spot for this.)

Chapter Two

Summary

1. Your anchor is your reason for why you "should" and "need" to make the necessary changes to begin building health.

2. Your anchor will keep you on track when times get tough.

3. Craft your anchor and read it daily to set your anchor, letting it go from your head to your heart.

Your Turn

1. What has stopped you in the past from making changes?

_____

_____

_____

_____

2. What has been your biggest nutritional obstacles in the past?

_____

_____

_____

_____

3. How will your anchor help you with those things you struggled with in the past?

_____

_____

_____

_____

Why 14 Days?

Young & Dumb

Have you ever had one of those moments you wish you could go back and do it over again? In my first nutritional consultation, I was sitting in front of my first patient, jotting down notes, taking in all her concerns, hurts, diseases, and goals. I went home with all the information, spending hours putting together a very detailed plan tailored just for her. After hours of planning and research, I walked into our next visit with a completed plan in a 1 ½-inch binder; it included protocols, charts, day-by-day instructions, etc. It was pretty much everything I had learned in all my years of schooling, packed into a binder ready to be explained in 30 minutes. I saw the deer-in-the-headlights look, but I forged ahead. As a side note, I am Puerto Rican; and if you know anything about Spanish people, we have an uncanny ability to speak very fast...I think it's genetic. So yes, I was able to go through my 1 ½- inch binder in record time. I even had time left to answer questions. Yes, the plan I put together would work...if she had the discipline of a Navy Seal!

Honestly, it was a very difficult, year-long plan to follow. Most of the people who would go through the plan would see great results early, but couldn't make it the full year. All of the patients would quit the plan, or worse, wouldn't start at all. I was essentially recommending that people change their entire lives from the 30 minutes of information I threw at them. Yeah, that worked well. [Insert eye rolling or deep sigh here.]

Searching for Answers

My intentions were right, my heart was all in, but my system wasn't working. Frustrated with my lack of results, I began to understand the attraction to and reason people do FADs, fast diets, and are looking for the magic pill. So, I started looking into 90-day programs; and after much research, I created one for my patients. Many people were compelled to do it for 90 days; and those who completed the program would get great results. But then in time, they would go right back to their old lifestyles and their old habits. So I went back to the drawing board; and from the 90-day plan, I created a 30-day plan for my patients, finding that each time I decreased the length of the plan, I saw the rate of compliance rise. More people were able to finish the plans, and I continued to see really great results. However at the end of my plans and recommendations, old lifestyles would creep in; and the results would wear away.

MED

Minimum Effective Dose (MED) – In his book, *The 4-Hour Body*, Tim Ferriss defines MED as "the smallest dose that will produce the desired outcome." A great example he uses involves boiling water:

If you want to boil water, all you need to do is heat the water to 100° Celsius (212°F) at sea level. That is the MED to boil water. If you heat the water to 105°C, the water does not get more boiled. Anything above 100°C just wasted more resources to get your desired result of boiling water.

After I read this, I started thinking how I could apply this concept to a nutritional lifestyle. Hold that thought as we continue looking at the research

When My Mind Shifted

As I continued my research, I found an amazing study that was done on a group of people who live in the Marshall Islands, in the Pacific Ocean.

Chapter Three

In WW2, the United States used these islands for nuclear bomb testing. Prior to this testing, the people of the Marshall Islands rarely experienced any of the chronic lifestyle-induced diseases that we see here in the U.S. They had minimal to no diabetes, cancer nor heart disease. When the testing was over, it was determined that the nuclear bombs had destroyed some of the vegetation. Because of this destruction, the U.S. wanted to help them rebuild what was damaged. We began sending them some of our processed foods. In a very short time, the people of the Marshall Islands went from having no type 2 diabetes to having the highest per capita cases of type 2 diabetes in the world. The cancer and heart disease rates began to rise as well, putting the residents of these islands on a downward spiral of health.

In 2005, Canvasback Missions Inc, a nonprofit Christian organization specializing in medical missions to remote South Pacific islands, was awarded a grant for a lifestyle intervention diabetes research study. This study, conducted in partnership with the Marshall Islands Ministry of Health and Loma Linda University, was launched in March 2006. During the study participants experienced the following results after a change in nutrition[1]:

- Fasting blood glucose declined by an average of 50-100 points

- Cholesterol dropped 20 points

Why 14 Days?

- Triglycerides decreased about 40 points

- Joint and limb pain decreased dramatically

- Needed medications decreased dramatically

These amazing results beg the question, "How long did it take for those changes to develop?"

You might have guessed it...only 14 days. In just 14 days these people were beginning to get their lives back. I used the concept of the MED (minimal effective dose to get a desired result) in developing the 14-Day Reboot. I also wanted to put a program together that was simple and doable for everyone. All of us can do two weeks.

Here is something cool. When you get a cut, or if you are fighting a head cold, on average, how long does it take your body to heal? Usually, 14 days is what it takes to fully heal a cut or a cold[2, 3]. That is why I am pumped about the 14-Day Reboot; it's easy and it works with your body's MED for healing to begin taking place. Now, not every disease and every ailment you are experiencing will go away in 14 days. However, you will begin the healing process. You will begin to rebalance hormones, lose weight, and detoxify your body.

Chapter Three

The "side effects" from our plan will be:

- Increased energy

- Increased mental sharpness

- Better sleep

- Weight loss

- Stronger immune system

These are just a handful of benefits you will experience as you implement your 14-Day Reboot.

From FAD to Lifestyle

The 14-Day Reboot solved one of the biggest issues I struggled with early in practice-- long-term compliance. Two weeks we all can do, but this did not solve the issue of old habits creeping back into my patients' lives. This is exactly why I have created the 14-Day Reboot and the Reboot Lifestyle Plan. In the book we will discuss and detail the Reboot and FuN nutritional plans and how you will take this from just another FAD diet to a true lifestyle plan.

Summary

1. Minimal Effective Dose (MED) – is the minimum requirement to see a desired outcome.

2. The 14-Day Reboot is not only simple, but it is effective because it gives your body the MED for the healing process to begin.

3. The 14-Day Reboot and Reboot Lifestyle solve the problem of long-term compliance.

Your Turn

1. What current health challenges are you experiencing? List all symptoms you are currently experiencing, medications you are using and diagnoses you have received.

_____

_____

_____

_____

Chapter Three

2. What would life look like if you began to heal from some or all of what you have listed above? Begin creating a vision for yourself – be as detailed as possible; i.e., how will you feel, look, and what will you be able to do?

_____

_____

_____

_____

_____

_____

_____

_____

Health Quiz

Before you go to Section 2 here is a short quiz to see where you are and where you are heading on your health journey.

1. Are you currently taking any medications?

Yes - 0

No - 5

2. Are you currently taking any supplements?

Yes - 5

No - 0

3. Do you currently have or have you previously had cancer, heart disease, or diabetes ?

Yes - 0

No - 5

4. Do you have increasing fatigue, lack of stamina or loss of energy?

Yes - 0

No - 5

5. Have you received vaccines in the past, including flu shots?

Yes - 0

No - 5

6. Do you have a history of autoimmune disease or illness?

Yes - 0

No - 5

EXERCISE

7. Do you exercise? (multiple choice)

Yes . How often?

1-2 times per week - 5

3-5 times per week - 10

6+ times per week - 15

No - 0

BODY COMPOSITION

8. Have you recently attempted to lose weight without success?

Yes - 0

No - 5

YOUR MENU

9. Do you eat sugar or carbohydrates (i.e. sweets or bread)?

Yes

How often?

1-2 times per week (0)

3-5 times per week (-5)

6+ times per week (-10)

No - 5

10. Do you eat less than 5 servings of vegetables per day?

Yes - 0

No - 5

11. Do you use artificial sweeteners like Aspartame, Splenda, NutraSweet or Sucralose or consume foods that contain them?

Yes - 0

No - 5

12. Do you consume fried foods?

Yes

How often?

1-2 times per week (0)

3-5 times per week (-5)

6+ times per week (-10)

No - 5

13. Do you consume processed "deli" meat, bacon, sausage, or hot dogs?

Yes - 0

No - 5

14. Do you use canola oil, vegetable oil or margarine?

Yes - 0

No - 5

15. Are the majority of the dairy, meats, fruits and vegetables you consume conventionally grown/raised (non-organic)?

Yes - 0

No - 5

16. Do you drink soda/pop regularly?

Yes - 0

No - 5

17. Do you eat wild caught fish on a weekly basis?

Yes - 5

No - 0

18. Do you have trouble waking up and starting your day each morning?

Yes - 0

No - 5

19. Do you feel like you have reduced libido?

Yes - 0

No - 5

HAIR, SKIN & NAILS

20. Do you suffer from dry skin, dermatitis, eczema, and/or psoriasis?

Yes - 0

No - 5

SLEEP

21. Do you have difficulty sleeping, experience nervousness or hyperactivity?

Yes

How often?

1-2 times per week (0)

3-5 times per week (-5)

6+ times per week (-10)

No - 5

PAIN

22. Do you suffer from chronic pain, joint pain or muscle aches?

Yes - 0

No - 5

23. Do you have headaches or migraines?

Yes - 0

No - 5

DIGESTION

24. Do you have digestive concerns (i.e. bloating, pain, gas, nausea, burping, heartburn or excessive body odor)?

Yes - 0

No - 5

MIND

25. Do you worry, feel stressed, anxious or overwhelmed, especially in typically low stress situations?

Yes - 0

No - 5

Tally your score by adding up the totals of your answers. See what your score means below:

100 - 125 = You are Rocking it!

This means you are making some great choices. Keep reading this book to continue rocking your health journey.

75 - 99 = Thumbs Up

This means you have made some healthy choices, but there is always room for improvement. I know this book will give you tools and strategies to make it easier and not harder to continue progressing on your health journey.

25 - 74 = No One is Perfect

This means either by lack of knowledge or lack of inspiration you have been making poor choices on your health journey. The fact that you are reading this book tells me something inside you wants to change. I hope this book is the catalyst for that change. You are the person I wrote this book for, because I have been there myself.

How did you score?

Date: _____   Score: _____

Date: _____   Score: _____

Date: _____   Score: _____

Date: _____   Score: _____

Date: _____   Score: _____

Once you're finished reading this book, come back to this section and set a goal based on the information you learn about your body's ability to heal itself and your control over you.

Remove the Bad; Rebuild with the Good

This section walks you through the steps your body needs to go through to not just thrive, but soar. The process is simple but challenging. Now that you have an anchor for the journey, it's time to get "smart" about your health. These chapters are filled with the knowledge needed to make great decisions. I've included lists, graphs, and visuals to really put the wind behind your sail.

The goal is to become
"fuel flexible"
— when our bodies have
the ability to easily
switch between
sugar burning
and fat burning.

The Process: Remove/Rebuild

My wife and kids love to watch *Nailed It*. On this reality series amateur bakers compete by trying to replicate a master baker's complicated cake and confectionery in order to win a $10,000 cash prize and the *Nailed It* trophy. The participants have all been given the necessary ingredients and tools for the job to be done correctly. The best part is at the end of the show, when they display their works of art and compare them to the original creation. And in most cases, they look nothing like the original. My whole family gets a kick out of the disasters the amateur bakers make.

You and I have probably fallen into this same trap with our health. We have learned all the information, we have all the right tools, we may have even tried all the right strategies for our health; but at the end we have seen little or no results. WHY? The answer is simple. Like the amateur bakers who have all the correct tools and ingredients to replicate the cakes properly, you still lack a critical component. The missing piece to the puzzle for success is having the process and professional guidance to get the job done correctly.

This is exactly why I have put together the 4-step Remove/Rebuild Process. Way too often I have seen people spend countless amounts of money, time and effort trying to get healthy, trying to lose weight, trying to re-balance their hormones, trying to (plug in your health goal), with minimal results. The Remove/Rebuild Process works because it gets to the root cause(s) of your struggles. For all of us, whether we like it or not, whether we believe it or not, our hormones play a vital and essential role in keeping us healthy. Hormones regulate virtually every metabolic pathway in your body. These pathways control all aspects of cellular health and activity; and, depending on how balanced your hormones are, this will directly affect how healthy you are. While I could continue and explain the details behind these paths and hormones, I will spare you the details since this book is not intended to be a class in biochemistry; this book is for you to get results and to get them fast.

In the next few chapters I have attempted to simplify my explanations of the inner workings of the body to what I believe is essential to understanding the big ideas and concepts without unnecessary biological details. I have added some illustrations and metaphors so you can have a more clear understanding of the importance of each individual step in the process. As you read the material, please keep in mind the following:

I was intentional in being general. When it comes to our complex bodies, "one size does not fit all" as they say, so certain examples and statements do not apply to all cases and individuals.

I did not want to make this a textbook with a lot of facts and figures. I want this to feel more like a conversation; as if you and I were sitting having a conversation about health.

I have also tried to answer many of the questions I have received over my years in practice, but I know there will be others that arise which I have not answered. I will make myself and my team available to answer questions and provide further guidance. You can reach us at **the14dayrebootbook.com** .

The Lies

We have all bought into the lie that losing weight and being healthy are all about calories in and calories out. This is a simple and logical concept that has been propagated for decades by our society but unfortunately, it's just not true. While calories do play a role in the process, the more important question

Chapter Four

is, what kind of hormonal response is your body having to the type of calories consumed?

If I were to have you eat 100 calories of a donut or100 calories of raw almonds, would this cause two radically different hormone responses in your body? Yes!

100 CALORIES   100 CALORIES

INSULIN – is the hormone responsible for maintaining proper blood glucose (sugar) levels. As blood glucose rises, your body releases more insulin to make sure blood glucose stays within a normal range.

The donut would cause a rapid elevation of insulin which would cause a cascade reaction affecting hormones such as cortisol (stress hormone), ghrelin (hunger hormone), and leptin (satiety and fat usage hormone), to name a few. This is a normal and proper response in the body, and the process is there to protect you. If the glucose level in your blood remained elevated or climbed too high, it could have devastating effects, including conditions which may cause death. To save you from this your body deals with any excess glucose by storing it. Can you guess how it stores it? You may have guessed it—as fat.

Eating the 100 calories of almonds, on the other hand, will affect the same hormones; but instead of causing insulin to rapidly elevate, it will cause a more gradual and stable insulin response. This response begins to have a hormone balancing effect on the body. As you can see eating is not just about calories, but the response your body is having to the types of calories. Eating the right foods can help you by prompting your hormones to work for you and not against you. Instead of focusing on the amount of calories we consume, we will focus on the quality of the calories and the effect those calories have on your hormones.

Hormonal Balance

When I talk about "hormonal balance" I am referring to the state at

Chapter Four

which proper hormones are being produced and effectively communicating throughout the body. You will see in reading the next few chapters how vitally important hormones are and how they support many functions in our bodies. When our bodies are under constant stress and pressure from our environment, over time our hormones may begin to over or under produce, or to miscommunicate all together. Our 4-Step Remove/Rebuild Process is designed to attack the four main triggers causing hormonal imbalances. These four triggers specifically target the hormones and the hormone receptor sites critical to metabolism and weight gain.

Fuel Flexibility

We have four crazy kids at home. By crazy, I mean beautiful. Watching them develop as babies has been amazing; they would get cute and chunky, then they would hit a growth spurt and thin out. I saw this happen with all our kids. They would fatten up, then thin out several times as they developed. I would think to myself, "I wish I could burn fat like they do." Babies and hormonally balanced kids are what I call fuel flexible, and that should be our goal.

Fuel flexible is when your hormones have the ability to easily switch between sugar burning and fat burning. Early on most of us have this fuel flexibility to switch between these two energy systems in our body. But, as we begin to eat the typical standard American diet, which is high in processed foods and toxins, we begin to depend more on our sugar/carbohydrate-burning system and less on our fat-burning system for energy. In some cases we completely shut down the ability to burn fat for energy.

You know you have become a sugar burner when…

- You constantly crave carbs and sugars

- You are having mood swings or often get "hangry"

- You struggle with belly fat

- You arc hungry shortly after eating

- You constantly feel tired

- You sleep and still feel tired

- You struggle with mental clarity and focus

- You walk by a donut shop and gain weight just by looking at the donuts (Yes, that's a joke.)

Chapter Four

These are just a few warning signs that you have lost your fuel flexibility and are relying primarily on sugars for energy. When we rely on sugars, our hormones tend to be out of balance, with massive swings up and down. These up and down swings in our hormones cause many of the warning signs above and are an indication that you are ready for a Reboot.

The Goal

The goal is to become Fuel Flexible. Over the next four chapters I outline the 4-Step Remove/Rebuild Process helping you achieve that flexibility.

The 4-Step Remove/Rebuild Process:

- **Step 1**- Remove Sugars

- **Step 2**- Rebuild with Fat

- **Step 3**- Remove Toxins

- **Step 4**- Rebuild with Protein

While I highly recommend reading the next four chapters, if you are looking to jump head first into your Reboot, go directly to Chapter 15, which explains the plans. Section three defines how to put the plan into action.

However, I suggest you come back and read the four chapters to have a greater understanding of what is happening internally.

Summary

1. We have two primary sources of energy: sugars and fats. Many of us over time begin to rely primarily on our sugar burning system. In many cases this causes hormonal imbalances which need to be addressed before major health complications occur.

2. The goal is to become "fuel flexible"—when our bodies have the ability to easily switch between sugar burning and fat burning.

Your Turn

1. Do you have any of the warning signs of sugar dependency from the list? If so, write them here.

_____

_____

_____

Chapter Four

What are some struggles and symptoms you feel mentally and physically that make you feel you are not fuel flexible?

_____

_____

_____

_____

_____

2. Looking at your answer to #2, what do you want to see a personal breakthrough with? Better sleep? Less fatigue? Balanced mood?

_____

_____

_____

_____

_____

5 Remove Sugars

Lock and Key?

Before we jump into the importance of this first step, I think it is important to have a general understanding of how hormones work in the body and what they do. Hormones are chemical messengers which travel through your body coordinating complex processes like growth, metabolism, fertility, immune system response, moods and many other functions. These chemical messengers work by activating specific cells or groups of cells. This activation occurs through very specific receptor sites. Each hormone has very specific receptor sites on the particular cells it needs to activate. To simplify this think of it as a lock and key arrangement.

If I pulled up to my house and walked up to the front door, I would expect the lock to open with my key. My key is, and should be, specific to my front door. Relating this to hormones, in this example, my key would be the hormone and the lock on my front door would be the receptor site. When my key goes into the lock it allows me to open my door and get into my house. Essentially, my key (the hormone) activates the lock (receptor site) and the desired response is that I am able to open my front door. In our bodies when hormones reach their specific receptor sites, it causes the cell to react a certain way; it may allow needed material into the cell, it may allow certain molecules to be released from the cell, it can activate growth or a myriad of other cellular responses, all which would be dependent on the particular hormone/receptor being studied. I hope this gives you a clearer picture of how hormones work in the body; here is the problem.

There are a lot of people who have been told or feel they have a "hormone problem." In reality, it is not a hormone problem; it is what I call a communication issue. Typically the body is still able to produce the specific hormones needed, but the body/cells are not producing the desired response. The problem is that more often than not, its not a hormone problem, it is a receptor issue. Receptor sites are prone to damage, and there are many factors which can damage them; but there are two main causes. The number one cause of damage to our receptor sites is eating too much sugar over extended periods. The second cause, which we will discuss in more detail in chapter 7, is the effect toxins have on our hormones.

When receptor sites are damaged our bodies have a "communication issue." Our bodies are still producing the desired hormone—trying to talk to and communicate a specific message to the cells; but, because of the damaged receptor sites, the cells are unable to receive the message. It is like my walking up to my house and trying to unlock my front door, but my key will not go into the lock because someone has damaged the lock. What most would call "having a hormone problem" is in fact having a receptor site problem, a "communication issue."

Can I Heal?

As someone begins to understand the hormone/receptor site relationship in the body, the next question they usually ask is, "Can receptor sites be healed?" Essentially, they are asking, "Can you heal this?" In section 1, we discussed the amazing healing power in each one of us. And our job was to remove what is causing interference to the natural healing power within our bodies and allow them to do what they do best--heal. The short answer to the above question is, YES, your body can heal; but it starts by removing the

Chapter Five

main culprit of receptor site damage: sugar. When we do this first step, we are truly getting to the cause and kick starting our body's healing mechanism and beginning the Reboot Process.

What Do I Mean by Sugar?

When teaching people that step one in our process is to remove sugar, most people respond by saying, "But I don't eat sugar." Maybe so, but when I say 'sugar' I mean anything that 'is' sugar or 'will turn into' sugar rapidly in your body. For example, as soon as something like bread goes into your mouth, you have certain salivary enzymes that immediately begin to break the bread down into usable sugar. Am I saying you will never be able to have bread again on our plans? No, I have bread rather frequently; but it must be a healthy, healing option; we'll get to that soon.

I promised that in this book I would make it easier and not harder for you when it comes to nutrition. The main concept that I want you to understand in this chapter is that, while we want to remove sugar during certain times in our plans (anytime we want to heal our bodies – as in the 14-Day Reboot period) all sugars are not created equal.

Essentially, when we are discussing sugar, we are discussing carbs.

Carbohydrates are a hot topic in the health world these days. On one hand you will hear how great they are for working out and for the function of your metabolism; but then, as discussed above, we can see how they can wreck our systems and hormones. This has left many people confused on the topic... and for good reason. I can see how the information is confusing and misleading. There are many trendy diets on the market these days, like the "Keto Diet", which can leave you feeling like carbs should be completely avoided. While that might be merited in some cases, it is not the case for everyone. Even when doing a keto diet, carbs are and should be part of the plan. The reality is it depends on the type and amount of carbs we are consuming.

The Low Down on Carbs

So, what exactly is a carbohydrate? Carbohydrates are your body's quickest form of energy. I compare it to the kindling when starting a wood fire. While the kindling might burn easily and rapidly, it requires you to put more on until the main power source (the wood) begins to burn. This is similar to our eating foods high in carbs; we may get a burst of energy, but it is quickly followed by an energy slump. Following the slump in energy is when we typically experience the most cravings for high carb and sugary foods. When we consume carbs, our digestive systems break them down into glucose, which is what your body will then convert and use as its primary fuel source. Remember from our previous chapter, our goal is to be "fuel flexible" our bodies have the ability to easily switch between using carbs and fat for fuel. We do not want our bodies constantly dependent on carbs, which may easily lead to hormone imbalance. When our bodies are "fuel flexible," we allow our hormones to work for us and not against us.

Carbohydrates can be broken down into three distinct categories: sugars, long-chain glucose and fibers. Let me quickly explain these.

- **Sugars** are sweet, small-chain glucose, usually seen on ingredient lists as glucose, sucrose, fructose, galactose and pretty much anything else ending in 'ose.' These are typically broken down very quickly, beginning in your mouth, and have the greatest effect on your hormones. These are also the most processed forms of carbs--white bread, pasta and corn syrup would be examples of highly processed and refined carbs.

- **Long-chain glucose** is broken down in the digestive tract; examples include brown rice, sweet potatoes, quinoa and others. These tend to be less processed and will not have as great an effect on hormones. As you will see in our FuN plan, these are the carbs I recommend.

- **Fibers** are from foods like avocados, berries, coconuts, figs, artichokes, black beans and chickpeas. Fiber rich foods are typically very well tolerated and cause the least amount of effect on your hormones. The fiber in foods is not absorbed by the digestive tract and actually supports good healthy bowel movements.

Distinguishing between what we call "healing carbs" and "damaging carbs" is simple. Whole, unprocessed carbs naturally containing fiber are the best sources of carbs; these we consider to be healing carbs. Any carbs that have been minimally altered by man and have their nutrients intact would be considered healing carbs. When we discuss our FuN Plan and Reboot Plan, we'll go over which carbs are approved within each plan.

Damaging carbs are ones that have minimal or no fiber present. They are called refined carbs, meaning they have been altered in a process that has removed most of their nutrients and fiber. Refined carbs are foods like white pasta, white rice, fruit drinks, pastries and, of course, plain sugar.

Your body responds very differently to healing carbs vs. damaging carbs. Damaging carbs lead to hormone instability, increased inflammation, increased rates of heart disease, cancer, diabetes and many other lifestyle conditions. The encouragement here is that, as long as we search for and take care of causes

Chapter Five

and never just treat and cover up symptoms, we give the body the best chance at healing. Knowing the ill effects of damaging carbs and sugar--knowing they are one of the main causes of or at the root of so many health conditions--is why removing them from our diets is Step 1 in our Remove/Rebuild Process.\

Pressing the Easy Button

I did promise I would make this easier and not harder, so in Chapter 13 - Making it Easier, Not Harder I discuss the concept of lateral shifts. Lateral shifts are easy shifts—easy side steps from things you are already doing--to make what you are already doing healthier. A great example would be instead of using sugar in your tea, coffee or homemade desserts, you laterally shift to stevia or xylitol. This is an easy shift that anyone can make. In that chapter, I have also added a list of lateral shifts for many common foods. To make this really simple, instead of having to remember lists and charts, at the end of each step of the Remove/Rebuild Process I will give you one question. This question will allow you to make the best choice for that step in the process. After reading these chapters, all you need to remember is four simple questions; and if you can answer those questions when you are choosing a food item, you can be assured you are making a great choice.

The Question

Does this food have any added sugars? The answer to this question should be "No." The question is simple; but what we are asking with this question is, has man altered the product by adding any processed sugars to it. When reading ingredients, follow our label reading guidelines in chapter 13.

Example:

While a strawberry has sugar naturally occurring in it, it does not have any added sugars. Strawberries would be approved because they have not been altered by man.

Strawberry Jam could be approved, but in many cases some producers may add sugars to make it taste sweeter. This is why it is important to read labels for ingredients. Strawberry jam without added sugars would be approved because it is minimally processed.

Summary

1. Step 1 in our Remove/Rebuild Process is to Remove Sugar. Remove as many added sugars to any food items you will be consuming.

Chapter Five

2. The reason this is a critical first step is because of the negative effect sugar has on our system. It will affect hormone patterns, increase inflammation and increase the rate of the most common lifestyle-induced conditions, i.e. heart disease, cancer, diabetes, etc.

3. Ask yourself the simple question, *"Does this food item contain added sugars?"* If you answer "no" then you are on a good track to begin your Reboot.

Your Turn

1. Go into your refrigerator/pantry and begin to familiarize yourself with products you buy which are filled with added sugars.

_____

_____

_____

_____

2. Begin teaching your kids about "Healing Carbs" and "Damaging Carbs" and how your family will be switching to more healing carbs.

_____

_____

_____

_____

3. At this point we are just getting familiar with what to look for; we are not making any drastic changes. Later in this book I will teach you how to make the switch easy. Here, list items you enjoy for which you would like to find healthy switches.

_____

_____

_____

_____

Chapter Five

6 Rebuild with Fat

Step 2 – Rebuild with Fats

Eating fat makes you fat. This is another lie that has been sold to us since the late 1970s when the low-fat craze began to take over America. It was thought that fat was the underlying cause of many of the sicknesses and diseases Americans were beginning to experience. However, while food manufactures took more and more fat out of our foods, the more obese we became. As the obesity epidemic rose, so did our rates of heart disease, diabetes and cancer. Today in America we have more low-fat foods than ever, yet we are more obese than ever.

If eating fat does not make us fat, then what does?

It all has to do with our hormones. If you are having trouble losing weight, the culprit may be weight loss resistance, aka leptin resistance. This is seen in those who have tried it all; they've been at the gym for months, they have drastically changed their diets, they have committed and yet see little to no results. This is typical for those who suffer from weight loss resistance.

Amber

Amber gained 18 lbs. after her second childbirth. A few years after the second child was born she decided to get rid of the extra weight. So she committed to getting back in the gym, every day doing cardio and weight training. The weeks went by and she had lost only four pounds. She was frustrated and feeling very stuck. She didn't understand why she couldn't lose the weight because she was doing everything right and was working very hard. She was also following a strict eating plan that included low-fat foods. What she didn't know was that she was suffering from weight loss resistance.

Weight loss resistance is a hormone communication issue. It is when your body is unable to communicate to the brain and trigger your body to burn fat for energy. (I hope this sounds familiar from our lock and key discussion in our previous chapter!) The "key" in this case would be the hormone leptin. Leptin is the chemical messenger which travels to and communicates with your brain to burn fat for energy and tells you to stop eating. In Amber's situation, the leptin hormone was not communicating properly in her body. So, even though physically she was doing a lot of good for her body by working out and eating healthier foods, if she didn't correct this "communication issue" between leptin and her brain; she was going to continue to struggle and see little to no success.

The Leptin Dilemma

Leptin is a hormone that regulates energy and suppresses appetite in the body. It does so because the amount of leptin in your body is directly related to the amount of fat cells in your body. Leptin travels to the brain and communicates to the hypothalamus. It tells our brains that we have enough fat (energy) in our bodies, and we should stop eating; or if we are running low on fat (energy), we need to eat to avoid starvation. The problem, as we learned in the previous chapter, is we could be causing damage to the receptor sites; and no matter how much leptin is being produced by our fat cells, the brain may not be getting the message. The lock and key arrangement is damaged and not working. This was Amber's issue and the issue I have seen many struggle with throughout my career.

This brings us back to the purpose behind our Remove/Rebuild Process. The process is intended to rebalance your hormones and allow your body to

Chapter Six

naturally reboot your health. In Step 1 we began to remove sugar, which is the number one culprit of hormone instability. As we remove sugar we begin to give the body a chance to stabilize the hormone response. In turn we also give the body a chance to begin to use fat for fuel and not to rely solely on carbs for energy.

Fat for Fuel

To begin the process of becoming "fuel flexible" we need to rebuild the body's pathways which use fat for energy. This is where the keto diet has been highly successful. In a ketogenic diet, people are successfully able to go from using carbs as their primary fuel source to using fats for energy. During our 14- Day Reboot, we will give you step-by-step instruction on how to begin rebuilding these pathways.

Here is the concept we need to understand and why the low-fat diet failed us. If we are to be fuel flexible, we need to easily have the ability to switch between using carbs and using fats for our energy; and this is driven directly by our food intake and the corresponding hormone response. The problem many times is we are told to, or have tried to, go on a low-carb diet and fail. Why do we fail? We fail because we are typically not taught to increase our intake of the vital fats that will drive and begin to activate the fat-burning pathways.

Think about this. If you instantly take away your primary fuel source (carbs) but at the same time continue to eat a prescribed low-fat diet, where is your energy going to come from. We have been so ingrained that fats are bad that even when we are eating lower-carb foods, we also make sure they are low in fat. Think low-fat milk, low-fat yogurt, lean meats, etc. This is nonsense. You literally begin to starve your body of the energy necessary to function. You have taken its primary source of energy away (carbs) and now you are not fueling it with the needed fats to rebuild and use for energy. It's no wonder after a few days of low-carb dieting, your body rebels against you and begins the massive craving for sugar, which drives you to give up before you've gained any traction. I hope you can see why fats are critical in this process, but all fats are not created equal.

The Truth About Fats

As fats became a component we needed to avoid, no one talked about how critical fats are to the proper functioning of our bodies. Fat helps your body absorb nutrients, and it helps maintain your body's core temperature. Some vitamins rely on fat to assist them in being absorbed. They work together as a team. Vitamins A, D, K and E are called "fat soluble" vitamins. These core vitamins are an essential part of your diet, and work hand in hand with fats for your body. Fats are also filled with many benefits that support your brain and nervous system. Fun fact: Your brain consists of mostly fat; so when you eat good healthy fats, you can say you are feeding your brain. Fats are also the basic components for building many hormones and hormone pathways in your body. The key to rebuild these pathways is that they must be healthy fats, as damaged fats clog these pathways and cause further metabolic dysfunction. Think of it as water going down a drain; if the drain is clogged with gunk, the water backs up and does not flow properly. This could be very annoying; and over time, it gets worse until you unclog the drain. You can think of damaged fats as gunk in your metabolic pathways; and the more you use them, the worse the issue gets. Healthy fats unclog these pathways and rebuild your metabolism. Healthy fats also help control food cravings between meals, whereas carbs and damaged fats fill you up for only short periods. How do you know what's damaged and what's not?

Healthy Fats vs. Damaged Fats

The one question you will ask yourself for Step 2 in our process is, "Does this food have healthy fats or damaged fats?" The simplest way to distinguish between fats is by answering the question I ask myself a often. Was this fat God made or man made? The more natural and less altered the fat the healthier it is for you. Healthy fats are the ones that you get from avocados and oils like coconut and olive oil. Raw dairy is also another great source of healthy fats. Raw milk from grass-fed cows, ghee, pure butter, and raw cheeses are all good options to add to your diet. If you want any of the benefits from fats, you have get them from the right sources. Here is a list of man-made vs. God-made fats and oils.

Be Careful

When shopping we need to be aware of tricky fats. I think it is pretty well known that trans fats, hydrogenated or partially hydrogenated oils are all man made and are included in the damaged fats list, which will damage our metabolism. However, there are a few tricky ones you may not be aware of; but as you can see in the chart, they are on the man-made/damaged list.

Canola Oil While Canola oil might seem natural and can be found in a lot of "natural" or "health food" items, it is a man-made oil that comes from rapeseed. When the rapeseed oil is extracted, it unfortunately contains lots of erucic acid which, in high doses, is toxic to humans. In the 1960s Canadian agriculturalists produced a new version of rapeseed which had only trace amounts of the toxic acid; they called it "Canola" which stands for "Canada oil, low acid."

Chapter Six

Vegetable/Corn Oil – These oils might seem natural because they originate in plant form; but the extraction process for vegetable and corn oils is very unnatural, damaging the oils and making them very unhealthy for our cells.

Take Away

The take away from this chapter is that, even though it may seem unconventional to eat high-fat foods, it is an essential part to rebuilding the pathways that will help you be "fuel flexible." The key is distinguishing between healthy vs. damaged fats.

What happened with Amber?

After weeks of minimal results, I consulted with Amber and recommended she begin by adding a good dose of healthy fats to her regimen so she could begin to rebuild her fat-burning pathways. In 2 ½ weeks she lost 11 pounds. She was ecstatic and felt empowered, knowing how to help herself get healthy and stay healthy!

Summary

1. Step 2 in our Remove/Rebuild Process is to Rebuild with Fat. The purpose of this step is to help rebuild critical metabolic pathways that allow your body to become fuel flexible by using fat for fuel.

2. Most of us have been sold the lie that low fat is better. In this chapter we discussed the vital nature fats play in vitamin absorption, building hormones and a host of other functions. The critical step is differentiating between damaged fats and healthy fats. How do you know what's healthy and what's not? Simply ask yourself, "Is this fat man made or God made?"

3. Making it simple, "Does this food contain damaged fats or healthy fats?" If it contains damaged fats we should stay away from it.

Chapter Six

Your Turn

1. Go into your refrigerator/pantry and begin to familiarize yourself with products that you buy which are filled with damaged man-made fats and list them here.

_____

_____

_____

2. Next time you go shopping a great first step would be to buy a good amount of good healthy oils and fats to begin rebuilding your fat burning pathways. Write down three healthy oils and fats you can purchase this week.

_____

_____

_____

Go to **the14dayrebootbook.com**
and find a recipe with good healthy fats to try.

Remove Toxins

Bioaccumulation

Detoxification is one of those topics you can find a lot of information about, but you wonder, what is the best way to accomplish it? While the word itself can feel overwhelming and confusing, I will give you the tools and simple steps to easily begin the detox process. First, though, I want to give you the why. Trust me, this is important. Your body and your hormones will thank you.

To understand detoxing, we first have to discuss something called bioaccumulation. Bio-what? Exactly. This is a concept that affects every single cell in the body. It's one of those sneaky things that is hurting us, and most of us have no clue it is happening. If bioaccumulation is not addressed, it can lead to dysfunction and can be the main culprit in diseases like chronic bowel conditions, chronic headaches, sleep disturbances, neurological dysfunctions, autoimmune irregularities, skin troubles, and you guessed it...

hormone imbalance. It is a significant reason people struggle with lack of energy, sleep, focus and much more. It starts with bioaccumulation and ends with detoxing.

So, what is it? First, I'll explain what bioaccumulation is and why it's important; and then I will give you practical and easy ways to naturally detox your body. No, this will not be difficult switches; these are simple lifestyle changes that can help to reboot your body and allow you to regain your health. This chapter is for you no matter where you are on your health journey, because, in our modern culture, bioaccumulation is something with which we all struggle.

Bioaccumulation is the accumulation of toxins in an organism at a rate faster than the organism can release them.

Let me explain this with my favorite analogy. If you have a bucket, and you begin to pour water into the bucket and do not stop pouring water in, what occurs? Eventually the bucket will overflow. This is a visual example of how toxins accumulate in the body.

We are bombarded with toxins from a wide variety of sources—from our foods and drinks, our environment, the products we put on our skin, and so much more. As the exposure to these toxins continues, our bodies fill up and are unable to keep up with its natural detox process. Over time, the bucket (your body) will be so filled, it will overflow. That overflowing is a picture of how dysfunction begins and leads to disease, imbalances, and other toxin-related health concerns.

Here are a few of the possible side effects of toxicity: anxiety, fatigue, skin eruptions, acne, skin discoloration, fever, mucous, coughing, sneezing, severe digestive issues, trouble sleeping, restlessness, joint pain, organ

Chapter Seven

dysfunction, hair loss, glandular failure, brain malfunction, memory loss, brain fog, loss of sex drive, heart arrhythmias, high blood pressure, neurological tinnitus, disorders of the bowel and kidney trouble; and the list goes on and on. If you experience any of these or a combination of these symptoms, you are at a higher risk of being overloaded with toxins[1].

Toxins and Your Hormones

Toxins play a huge role in the way you look, the way you feel and, most importantly, the way your body functions every single day. What many do not consider is the role toxins play in your hormonal balance.

First, we have to think back to the lock and key analogy I mentioned in chapter five. I stated that, out of the many factors affecting your hormone balance and communication, there are two main culprits which cause the greatest effect. Number one was sugar, which causes hormonal spikes and eventually damages receptor sites. The second, and just as important, is the effect toxins have on receptor sites. Toxins damage receptor sites and disrupt hormone communication by either directly causing damage to the receptor site itself or by mimicking hormones in the body.

Many foods we consume today contain hormones. The dairy animals and livestock from which we get our food are typically injected with growth hormones that, once consumed, end up in our bodies and begin to do damage. In addition to these hormones, we are constantly using and are exposed to chemicals found in plastics (BPA), which are xenoestrogens. These xenoestrogens mimic human estrogen, and are so powerful, they are actually stronger than our own hormones. We also battle other toxins, styrene, benzene and heavy metals such as lead and mercury, to name a few. These can be found in everything from Styrofoam cups, lotions, cleaning products (personal and home), vaccines, our food supply and many other sources. Many Americans also take counterfeit hormones, such as birth control pills, once again contributing to your body being out of balance and needing a Reboot.

Step 3 - Remove Toxins

The bad news is we will never be able remove all the toxins our bodies come in contact with on a daily basis. The good news is we can have a detox process which can minimize the effects these toxins may have on our systems. The goal is to reduce the toxic bioaccumulation as much as possible and to support the systems created to help us detox.

Detoxing is a natural process.

God created our bodies with a detox system built right in. Skin pushes out bacteria and toxins when you sweat; your lungs expel carbon dioxide; your kidneys filter your blood and produce urine to remove impurities and bi-products; your intestines absorb necessary nutrients and with the unwanted they create waste; and your liver is always working to clear out toxins from your body. But in this culture, our organs are having a harder time keeping up due to the high demand placed upon them on a daily basis. Chronic stress, physical inactivity, high consumption of processed foods, lack of sleep, and unhealthy habits make it harder for your body to remove toxins efficiently. This is why we must be aware of *The Toxic Top 3*.

In our *What About Supplements? Chapter 11*, I will discuss how to support and accelerate the natural detoxing process through proper supplementation. But here are the toxic top three to be aware of and how to begin decreasing the toxic bioaccumulation.

Toxic Top Three

1. Medication – Yes, while in some cases medication may save someone's life, the fact is that every medication is a toxin; and as a toxin your body must deal with it. I am not telling you to go home and stop all your medications. My recommendation is to begin following The 14-Day Reboot and Reboot Lifestyle; and as your body begins to heal, talk to your doctor about which medications you can begin decreasing to lower your toxic load. I have seen thousands of patients, as they begin to live out this new lifestyle, be able to get off many medications.

2. Household Toxins – Our home should be a safe zone for our families. Unfortunately, every product with a caution label, a danger sticker or warning sign on it has chemicals which are toxic and damaging to our systems. The ones who are at most risk are kids due to their size and lack of overall organ development. The main offenders are detergents, soaps, household cleaners and any products used on our skin and/or in our mouths. While there are many harmful chemicals, here are three main ingredients to stay away from at all cost.

Diethanolamine (DEA) – DEA was found to cause carcinogenic activity when applied to skin on rats[2].

Propylene Glycol – is a powerful solvent used in antifreeze solutions and hydraulic fluids; it has been shown to be easily absorbed through the skin. Studies have shown it to cause kidney damage, liver abnormalities, skin cell growth, immune system deficiency and central nervous system depression[3].

Chapter Seven

Sodium Lauryl Sulfate (SLS) – has been shown to enter the heart, liver, lungs, and brain from skin contact and has been proven to maintain residual levels in these organs once it enters them causing damage[4].

All three of these are highly common and found in almost all home products that are not natural.

The solution here is to begin using natural products that do not contain these or other harmful chemicals. The good news is natural products can be found at most major retailers today.

3. Tap Water – Our water today contains toxins such as chlorine, fluoride, lead, arsenic, prescription medications, and atrazine. (This is a known hormone disruptor and has been linked to birth defects and shown to increase levels of estrogen in women, which can increase risk of breast and ovarian cancer. It has also been found to feminize frogs turning once-male frogs into females.) These are just a handful of the 316 chemicals found by the Environmental Working group in our country's tap water in a three-year study which concluded in 2009[5].

The solution here is not to drink water (Just kidding). Water is essential in our detox process. After much research the most cost effective and safest way to protect yourself and your family is to install a full house and/or point of use water filtration system.

For more information and resources, visit:
the14dayrebootbook.com

Toxic Foods

The premise here is the same as with the previous chapters, the more processed the food, the higher probability that the food contains materials which are toxic. When it comes to food a great rule of thumb is, if you can't pronounce the ingredients or if the ingredient has numbers in it you shouldn't eat it. Here is your one question for this chapter, "Does the food or product contain toxic chemicals?" These chemicals include anything from food additives, preservatives, colorings and yes, any fake sugars like aspartame (Equal), or sucralose (Splenda).

Are we able to follow this rule all the time? Well, not 100% of the time, but you have to remember the goal. The goal is reducing as much of the toxic exposure as possible. It will be impossible to live a 100% toxic-free life in our culture. But we can take many steps to reduce the exposure and protect

Chapter Seven

ourselves and our families; and you start by answering 'no' to the one question more often than not. Because no one can live a 100% toxic-free lifestyle. This is one of the main reasons my family and many of our patients are committed to the yearly reboot cycle. I will discuss this cycle in the Reboot Lifestyle chapter in section three. In section three I also discuss more details on when to buy organic vs. non-organic produce in the *Making it Easier, Not Harder* chapter.

Summary

1. Step 3 in our Remove/Rebuild Process is to Remove Toxins. Over time toxins will accumulate in our bodies and begin to cause damage. This is called toxic bioaccumulation.

2. The goal is not a 100% toxic free lifestyle which would be impossible in our modern culture. The goal is to be aware of the main offenders and reduce the toxic load as much as possible. This will allow your natural detoxification system to do its job and help your body heal and stay healthy.

3. Making it simple, "Does this food or product contain toxic chemicals?" If it does, we try to stay away from these products as much as possible.

Your Turn

1. Go into your refrigerator/pantry, cleaning space and bathroom and begin to familiarize yourself with products that you buy which are filled with toxic chemicals. Journal that list.

_____

_____

_____

_____

_____

Chapter Seven

2. Your step here is not to throw everything out and start new (although you can). The goal would be, next time you run out of a specific cleaning, personal or food product, that you would replace it with a new, non-toxic version. Write down **three products or more** you are about to run out of such as deodorant, face wash, toothpaste, household cleaner, etc., and find less toxic versions of this for you to try out, and hopefully switch to permanently.

_____

_____

_____

_____

8   Rebuild with Proteins

The Legos® of Your Body

Proteins are an incredible group of molecules in the body. They are responsible for so many roles. Proteins are formed from smaller structures, called amino acids. These are the building blocks of your body. Like Legos®, you can put together and build many different structures, amino acids can also be put together in different arrangements to take on thousands of different roles throughout your body. Making sure you are getting the proper amount of proteins and absorbing them correctly is vitally important. I'll discuss in detail more about absorption in the *What About Supplements* chapter.

Proteins have typically gotten a bad rap. When we hear the word "proteins" we usually think of protein bars and shakes, which most people associate with muscle building, working out, and meat heads. Perhaps that's not your train of thought, but it is mine. If you think that way, I want to help you see the bigger picture. Yes, proteins are used for building muscle, which we all need; but they do so much more. Proteins are used for transporting oxygen, repairing cellular damage, carrying nutrients throughout the body, holding genetic information, structural support, and building hormones and hormone receptor sites. [Ding, ding ding...this should set off an alarm.]

If you have been tracking with me over the last few chapters with our lock and key analogy, then check this out. I wrote in an earlier chapter that the body can absolutely heal as long as you take certain steps to remove what caused the damage to begin with. As explained before, we began to remove damaging sugars (carbs) and remove toxins which destroyed the receptor sites. The second part of rebuilding damaged hormones and hormone receptor sites is giving your body good healthy fats and proteins. This allows for the proper communication to begin to take place between hormones and cells. Most people know they are experiencing a problem with hormones, but they don't know where to start. I have found going through the 4-Step Remove/Rebuild Process is the best way for that rebalancing to take place, and this step is a critical part of the process.

Many hormones and mood regulating neurotransmitters are made up of proteins. At their core, insulin and leptin, which we discussed earlier, are proteins that regulate your blood sugar level, fat storage and satiety (tells your brain you are full). Melatonin and serotonin come from the breakdown of proteins, and are known to regulate sleep and happiness.

PROTEINS – *they break down into amino acids. There are 9 essential amino acids. They are essential because your body cannot synthesize them; we must get them from foods.*

If you are feeling out of balance, making sure you are getting the proper amounts of proteins is critical. If your body is deficient in certain amino acids—specifically the essential amino acids—you can see massive hormone, mood and cognitive imbalances. [In the upcoming chapter on supplementation, I will discuss available options for testing to see if you have vitamin, mineral and/or amino acid deficiencies.]

Healthy Proteins = Healthy Cells

I hope you are convinced that proteins are not only for those looking to gain muscles. Consuming proteins will not cause you to gain muscle and look like Arnold Schwarzenegger. (I had to look up that spelling!) Other factors are necessary to grow muscles like a body builder. While you won't grow muscles

Chapter Eight

simply by taking in proteins, a lack of protein can cause hormonal and mood imbalances, which may lead to overeating and fat retention. I'd rather be on the safe side and eat my proteins.

Proteins have so many amazing and important functions in our bodies; unfortunately, as with fats, all proteins are not created equal. There are healthy proteins and damaged proteins; and for your body to rebuild and work well, it needs the healthy ones. You've probably heard it said, "Good in, good out and junk in, junk out." This holds true here. If you consume damaged proteins you will have damaged cells and a damaged body; if you take in healthy proteins, you build healthy cells and a healthy body. So, we need to clearly identify which are good proteins and which are not. The main source of protein is our diet. We need to know what to look for when shopping for healthy proteins, whether from meat or plants.

Let's look at animal proteins first. What should our cows be eating? This is pretty simple—cows naturally roam and graze from the land, eating grass. Sadly, conventionally raised cattle, chickens and/or other livestock are fed corn and other industry by-products (like candy). These are not only unnatural substances for these animals to eat, but they are also filled with toxic medication and hormones to fatten the animals as quickly as possible for human consumption. In many cases these animals are kept inside buildings, some never seeing light, standing, sitting or lying in their own waste and subjected to other horrible conditions. Many of them cannot walk because they are being given so many hormones that their legs cannot support their growth rate and weight, and they collapse.

A saying we like to repeat around our house is, "You are what you eat, eats!" And we do not want to be filling our bodies with food that has been filled with toxins and hormones. Consider this: If you are eating meats that are filled with medications and hormones, you can pretty well guess what you are filling your system with.

I am a football fan. Recently, after a few players tested positive for substances they had never taken, the National Football League warned players about eating meats which may contain banned steroidal substances[1]. The investigation found that meats produced in Mexico and China had high levels of Clenbuterol, which in America is a banned performance-enhancing substance. I share this to demonstrate the amount of toxins contained in our meat supply. Because of the way these meats are produced and the high toxic load they contain, these would be considered damaged proteins, which we need to avoid at all cost. Any protein source, including seafood and poultry, that

Chapter Eight

comes from animals that are conventionally raised must be avoided.

What should we look for when buying meat, poultry and fish? Take note of our best to worst chart in the *Appendix*. Simply stated, we must look for animal proteins that are raised as naturally as possible. As is the case with most foods, the more man has altered the natural process of cultivation, or with animals, the way they are raised, the fewer benefits they have for the body.

Must My Proteins Come from Animals?

The answer here is, "Absolutely not!" You can get all of your proteins from plant sources, and there have been many studies to support the argument that plant-based diets are more beneficial to the human body. Here is my take on it. I have studied many different cultures and their eating habits. I looked at cultures that had the top percentage of elderly with the lowest rates of lifestyle diseases, like cardiovascular disease, cancers and diabetes. My point in doing this was to see if there was any commonality in what they ate. I thought, if I could find the common link within these different people groups, I will have found the perfect diet—for which so many of us have been looking. Unfortunately, that was harder than expected.

One culture, the Abkhazians[2], ate a high plant-derived diet with little meat. Another group were the nomads of Mongolia[3], who ate almost all meat and very little plant-based foods. This culture even consumed beer they fermented themselves. I found another group which ate mainly fish. My point is, after looking at many people groups, I found little to no commonalties in what they ate. What I did find, however, was out of all the groups and cultures I studied, none ate processed foods. Whether they were vegetarians, vegans, pescatarians, omnivore or any other combination, the foods they consumed were being produced as God had intended them to be produced, naturally. That is the key:

To eat the least possible amount of processed foods.

If people have a philosophical reason for eating a plant-based diet, I'm all for it. But if it is for health reasons alone, I do not think the evidence is clear that a plant-based diet is the answer. I do, however, believe that we Americans need to drastically increase out intake of plant-based foods. Because the effects from these processed food products are so damaging, if you are unable to obtain good, clean sources of animal products, I would recommend staying away from conventional proteins and moving to a more plant-based approach to eating.

Chapter Eight

If you do decide to use a plant-based approach, here are a few things to consider:

- Buy products that are Non-GMO (non-genetically modified).

- Buy Organic whenever possible.

- You must still read ingredients. Even though it's plant based, it may still contain other chemicals and additives.

- You must be diligent about combining foods to make sure you are getting all 9 essential amino acids.

- Nutritional testing would be essential to determine any possible amino acid deficiencies.

Go to **the14dayrebootbook.com** for more information on nutritional testing.

The Question

The question for this chapter is simple. Does this food contain healthy or damaged proteins? If it contains damaged proteins, stay away from it at all cost.

Summary

1. Step 4 in our Remove/Rebuild Process is to Rebuild with Proteins. Proteins are critical to the rebuilding process. Proteins break down to amino acids and are the building blocks of our bodies. These are critical in the building of cells, hormones, hormone receptor sites, bones, skin and many other structures in the body.

2. The key is to be able to differentiate between healthy proteins, which help you build a healthy body, and damaged proteins, which damage your body. When it comes to animal proteins, we must buy naturally-raised proteins and stay away from conventionally-raised proteins at all cost.

3. Making it simple, "Does this item/food contain healthy or damaged proteins?"

Chapter Eight

Your Turn

1. Think of the proteins your family consumes on a weekly basis and write down three different ones you could start buying that are healthy and not damaged.

_____

_____

_____

_____

2. How could you eat more protein throughout the day? (Think eggs for breakfast or hardboiled eggs for lunch, adding chicken to your salads.)

_____

_____

_____

_____

9

SAD, FuN Plan vs. Reboot Plan

Let's Eat

The dictionary definition of nutrition is "The process of obtaining or providing the food necessary for health and growth." I love a good definition, and what I love about this one is it explains the importance of eating the right foods for health and growth. That is how we need to look at food. Food is the fuel that moves you, the blocks to build you and the essential components to heal you. But our problem is that many of us, including me at times, eat based on our cravings—what we want to eat—and not based on what we need to eat.

Most people know having good nutrition is important; but some link good nutrition with deprivation, eating foods we don't like, eating foods that are too expensive, and many other negative associations. Over the next few sections, I will show you how that doesn't need to be the case; "you can have your cake and eat it, too" so to speak. The unfortunate thing is, while we have negative associations with eating healthy foods, we don't associate how our Standard American Diet (SAD) contributes to major dysfunctions leading to disease, loss of quality of life and early death. These diseases include heart disease, hypertension, forms of cancer, type 2 diabetes, osteoporosis, gall bladder disease, dementia, and many more. Why don't we make a change, then, since many of us realize this? One reason is we don't have a big enough anchor. (Make sure you read and apply Section 1.) The second reason is that healthy eating seems difficult, even overwhelming. No worries, I'm here to help you make it easy.

SAD

Most people eat SAD, which is the Standard American Diet. This is a diet that is high in conventional meats, conventional dairy products, processed foods and sugar, with a minimal intake of fruits, vegetables and wild-caught fish. Statistics have shown that 63% of America's calories come from processed foods, 25% come from unhealthy animal-based foods, and only 12% comes from plant-based foods1. This is the reason the Standard American Diet is abbreviated SAD. All hope is not lost, however; this is a ship we can easily turn around!

When you think SAD, think processed foods.

FuN Plan

Let's talk FuN, which is our Functional Nutrition Plan. FuN is how we should strive to eat for the rest of our lives; and it's the foundation of your new Reboot lifestyle. The FuN Plan allows you to eat all fruits, good healthy grains, all vegetables and naturally raised proteins. And, on the FuN Plan, you are also allowed vacation meals!

> **VACATION MEALS** - *the meals that allow you to "have your cake and eat it too." See the vacation meal explanation in Making it Easier, Not Harder chapter.*

Easy Button Questions

In the *Appendix* we have given you food charts and brief explanations outlining the approved food options for the FuN Plan. Before we dive into the details, let me remind you of the four questions to make this as easy as possible. Asking yourself these questions will give you the guidance necessary to begin making great food decisions.

- **Does this food contain added sugars?**
  Goal: to eliminate added sugars or processed carbohydrates.

Chapter Nine

- **Does this food contain damaged fats or healthy fats?**

  Goal: to eliminate all damaged fats and increase your intake of good healthy fats.

- **Does this food or product contain toxic chemicals?**

  Goal: to eliminate added preservatives, food colorings and added chemicals.

- **Does this food contain healthy or damaged proteins?**

  Goal: to eliminate conventional meats and add naturally raised meats.

When you think FuN Plan,
think minimally processed foods.

See the *Appendix* for approved FuN and Reboot food lists and charts.

Reboot Plan

While the FuN plan is how we should be eating all the time, the Reboot Plan is designed to do exactly what it says – Reboot our bodies. Think of the times when your computer or phone is not responding, and the only option you have is to press the magical reboot button to get it working again. This Plan is designed with healing in mind. It is geared to reboot your body by decreasing inflammation, re-balancing hormones, detoxifying your body and kick-starting your metabolism. It is also the Plan that allows for short-term, rapid weight loss management (if needed) by aiding your body in using fat for fuel and allowing you to become fuel flexible.

This short-term Plan is typically done for 14 days.

WHY 14 DAYS? *As mentioned in section one, 14 days is the MED (minimum effective dose) or time your body needs to allow for healing to begin.*

Although we have outlined this Plan to be done in 14 days, there may be people who are genetically suited to do this plan for longer periods of time. Also, if this is your first time going through the Reboot Plan, it may be advantageous to continue on the Plan until your desired health goals have been met, before switching to the FuN Plan.

What does the Reboot Plan entail? The reboot plan is what takes you from SAD to the FUN.

Chapter Nine

The Reboot is a little more challenging than the FuN Plan. Remember, though, it is only two weeks. You can do anything for two weeks. There are three rules on the Reboot Plan.

Remove all the sugary (carbs) interferences.

On the Reboot Plan, not only are we removing added sugars, we are also removing anything that turns into sugar rapidly in our system. This includes all grains, flours and high-sugar fruits and veggies. (Allowed fruits and veggies are outlined in the *Appendix*.)

Remove damaged fats and add lots of good healthy fats.

On the Reboot Plan, we are being diligent to add healthy fats, and making sure all damaging fats are eliminated. This will allow us to begin using fat for energy and become fuel flexible.

Remove damaged proteins and add healthy proteins.

On the Reboot Plan, we are eliminating all damaged proteins and adding healthy proteins to give are bodies the building blocks necessary to rebuild.

See the *Appendix* for approved FuN and Reboot food lists and charts.

When you think Reboot Plan,
think healing by eliminating carbs and vacation meals.

I know this might seem tough; but after working with thousands of patients from many different backgrounds, I am confident you can do this. The two weeks of the Reboot will have hard moments; but when those come, concentrate on your anchor. Your anchor is your reason for making the change. Having an accountability partner is also beneficial during the 14 days. The Reboot Plan will kick-start your healing, which is what you want and need. It's time to make the change and see the results you have always wanted. It's time to press the Reboot Button.

See chapter 15 for the *Reboot Plan and Daily Guide.*

Look for additional support and guidance at
the14dayrebootbook.com

Summary

1. The Standard American Diet (SAD) is a diet high in conventional meats, conventional dairy products, processed foods and sugar.

Chapter Nine

2. Eating this diet has led to an epidemic of lifestyle-induced diseases across America.

3. The FuN Plan is the way we should strive to eat for the rest of our lives and is the foundation of your new Reboot. When choosing FuN foods, think of the four easy button questions.

4. The Reboot Plan is the healing plan. While it is a bit more difficult, it allows your body to rebalance hormones, detoxify, lose weight and heal.

Your Turn

1. Now that you know the breakdown of the different diets, which one do you fall under? Do you eat a lot from the SAD diet?

_____

2. Pick three foods off of the reboot approved list and begin adding them to your diet.

_____ _____ _____

10

Accelerators

In our previous chapters, we covered the 4-Step Remove/ Rebuild Process. We also explored the differences between the FuN and Reboot Plans. In the following section we have put all of it together and show you step by step how to implement the Plans and make them a lifestyle. We're also including a shopping guide, sample recipe resources and other valuable content to make the journey easier for you. Before we jump to the next section, however, I want to share two very specific tools which will help accelerate your results during your 14-Day Reboot.

Each tool will be discussed separately, including examples of how to use them during and after the 14-Day Reboot. As you will see in the following sections, the 14-Day Reboot has beginner to advance versions. When you move from beginner to advance versions, you will notice I have layered in the accelerators making each version more effective, but also a bit more challenging.

Let's begin pressing the gas pedal on your results. On your mark, get set, go!

Tool # 1 - Intermittent Fasting (IF)

Many hear the term "fasting" and immediately think "starvation." This is not long-term fasting; it's intermittent fasting, which most of us do periodically anyway. Think of the word "breakfast." If you break down the word (break-fast) you will notice the word "fast." Each day, when you eat your first meal of the day you are "breaking" a "fast." Let's suppose you ate dinner at 6pm and did not snack after dinner; the next day, if you had breakfast at 8am, you have just fasted for 14 hours. This is exactly how intermittent fasting (IF) works. It is not starvation; it is a specific time where you choose not to eat to receive the benefits of fasting.

Fasting has many benefits; and we can use fasting in our favor to accelerate results during our 14-day Reboot or beyond, when we are on the FuN plan. Here are a few of the researched benefits of IF [1, 2, 3, 4, 5, 6]

- Rebalanced hormones

- Improved mental clarity and concentration

- Weight and body fat loss

- Lowered blood insulin and sugar levels

- Reversal of type 2 diabetes

- Increased energy

- Improved fat burning

- Increased growth hormone

- Lowered blood cholesterol

- Gut healing (time of rest)

- Activation of cellular cleansing by stimulating autophagy, a discovery that was awarded the 2016

- Nobel Prize in medicine

- Reduced inflammation

Fasting is not a new concept. It has been around since ancient times.

Chapter Ten

Many cultures have fasted for health and spiritual reasons. As a Christian, I look at scriptures; and it is hard to miss the many different people who fasted, including Jesus (although I don't believe he fasted for health reasons). While they fasted for spiritual reasons in biblical times, for the purpose of this section, we'll stick to health. Here is a brief explanation of how fasting can help rebalance hormones and help you become more fuel flexible.

Our bodies store energy in two forms; one is glycogen (stored glucose). Glycogen is mainly stored in the muscles and in the liver. But we have a limited amount of glycogen storage. We store, on average, about 2000 calories of glycogen in our systems, or about 24-36 hours of energy from glycogen. When our systems are full of glycogen, the liver begins to transfer the excess energy to our second form of storage, fat.

High Carb Foods → Causes Insulin spikes →
Fills up liver and muscle glycogen storage → Leads to Fat Storage

High Carb Foods Increases Insulin (hormone spikes) Liver and Muscle Full of Glycogen Fat Storage

When we Intermittently Fast, we reverse the process and allow the body to begin using fat for fuel.

Intermittent Fasting → Hormones Rebalancing →
Depletes Glycogen in the Liver and Muscles → Fat Usage

There are many ways to use intermittent fast. Here are the two types of fasting I most commonly use:

16/8 Protocol

How It Works – During this type of fasting you eat only during an 8-hour window and fast for the remaining 16 hours. For most people this is easily done by skipping breakfast.

Using the example above:

If your last meal was at 7pm, the next morning you would skip breakfast and eat your first meal of the day at or after 11am = 16+ hours of fasting

Some people use the 16/8 protocol and shrink the eating window to 6 or even 4 hours. Either way the eating window is fluid. I would recommend testing a few different options to see what works best with your body and schedule. In the above example breakfast is skipped, but some people choose to skip dinner; you will need to see what works best for you.

Chapter Ten

During the fasting period, you consume no calories. However, black coffee, calorie-free sweeteners like stevia, tea and non-toxic, non-toxic sugar free gum is permitted. Oh yeah, and lots of water!

Pros – This tends to be the most flexible and easiest form of fasting, since you need to skip only one meal.

Cons – The eating window must be at the same time or you may lose some of the benefits. Also, because we store 24-36 hours of glycogen, it might begin the process, but might not get you to fat burning mode quickly.

14-Day Reboot – On the Intermediate and Advanced levels we use the 16/8 protocol daily for the 14 days. The goal is that the compounding effect will help accelerate the results and help you get to fat-burning mode quicker.

My Usage – After the 14-Day Reboot I use the 16/8 protocols on Monday, Wednesday and Friday mornings. This works well with my schedule, because I go into the office early on those days. Some people do this routine Monday – Fridays, some just once a week. You will need to see what works best for you. Your usage will be dependent on your goals.

24+ Fast

How It Works – During this fast you are fasting for 24+ hours. This may be done once a month or once a week. During the 24-hour fast, no food is consumed; but you can drink calorie-free beverages such as teas and coffee. When the fast is over, you go back to eating normally. This is pretty simple and self-explanatory.

Dinner at 6pm—No Eating Next meal at 6pm (if you are able to go to the next morning you will really receive the full benefit of the fast) = 24+ hours of fasting

Once again this is not an all-or-nothing approach. You should test and see how your body responds. If you get to only 20 hours on your first attempt, great. You will see after a few times it will get easier, and you will reap more of the benefits of IF. The goal is to give your body a break and allow it to rest, recover and heal.

Pros – This is the most effective way to kickstart the healing process. It is the best method to use glycogen reserves and begin burning fat for fuel, as well as the quickest way to begin rebalancing hormones and becoming fuel flexible.

Chapter Ten

Cons – Going 24 hours without any calories may be difficult, especially at first. Many people struggle with going extended periods of time with no food. You will want to end the fast with a lighter meal. I like to ease my way back to eating with a homemade bone broth. Be careful not to overeat after the fast which will negate some of the benefits of the fast.

14-Day Reboot – On the Advanced level of our Reboot, I have inserted a 24+ hour fast to begin prior to the 14-day Reboot. The goal is to kick-start your Reboot for maximum effectiveness. I would not recommend it for first timers, as you may experience headaches, tiredness, anxiousness, and other detoxing symptoms. I suggest you go through at least one Reboot to prepare your body before trying the Advanced version.

My Usage – After the 14-Day Reboot I typically use the 24+ Fast once a month. I also try to do it following a full day of vacation meals (which I explain in the *Making It Easier, Not Harder* chapter).

IF Notes

- Fasting should be intermittent; long-term fasting can be done under a physician's supervision.

Accelerators

- If you are pregnant or breast feeding, you should not fast.

- If you are on prescription medication, you should consult your physician before fasting

- If you have struggled with eating disorders in the past, I recommend seeing a physician before starting any type of fasting.

Here are some things to remember during your Intermittent Fast:

- Drink plenty of water—staying hydrated is key during any fasting and during the 14-Day Reboot.

- Stay busy—I have found it's easier for me to fast when I am busy at the office. Fasting at home on a weekend typically means failure for me.

- You may drink coffee or teas, but make sure they are organic and calorie free.

- Ride out the hunger waves—yes, you will get hungry, but the feeling will pass. Non-toxic gum and water are a major help.

Chapter Ten

- Try again—if you fail, that is okay; try again. It becomes easier as your body becomes more fuel flexible.

- Don't binge after fasting—overeating following your fast may negate the benefits you derived from it.

Tool # 2 – HIIT

High Intensity Interval Training (HIIT) is a very effective workout that keeps your body fuel flexible. The goal is to do an exercise that allows you to elevate your heart rate close to your maximum heart rate, and then follow it with a rest period. For example, you might run in place as fast as you can for 20 seconds and rest for 20 seconds. The work-to-rest ratio can vary depending on the intensity of your workout. Regardless of your fitness level, everyone can benefit from HIIT; and anyone can do it. Here are some of the benefits of HIIT:

- HIIT takes less time: Many people are overwhelmed by working out and going to the gym for an hour; but with HIIT, you can complete a session in as little as 5-15 minutes. Research has found that 4-minute HIIT intervals outperformed (energy usage, meaning weight loss) long-distance running by 10%[1]. Imagine, a 16-minute workout is more effective than a long-distance run of 30 minutes. The HIIT workout time is much more achievable and less overwhelming, regardless of your season of life.

- HIIT can be done anywhere, anytime and requires no equipment: You don't need a gym membership to do HIIT. You don't need any machines because your body is one. You can do HIIT at home, in your backyard, in your living room, at the park or even in your hotel room if you travel often. Because workouts are readily available online, you don't need to be creative or feel overwhelmed about how and what to do. Go to www.the14dayrebootbook.com and get a free pdf and videos of simple routines that can be done anywhere anytime.

- HIIT turns your body into a fat-burning machine: As discussed earlier, we have two main energy sources, fats and carbs; and we utilize them depending on the hormones which are produced. How we exercise produces a very specific hormone response. The key hormone here is Human Growth Hormone (HGH), which has many beneficial effects, including increasing your metabolism and helping you burn fat. Minimal amounts of HGH are produced when you do longer cardio sessions. HIIT sessions, in comparison to cardio sessions, drastically increase the production of HGH. Studies show that following a HIIT session, your body

Chapter Ten

can burn fat for the next 24-36 hours2. That is a great way to accelerate results!

Here is a simple HIIT session example I call "Simple, But Not Easy."

- Squats - 20 seconds on / 20 seconds rest (3 times)

- Push-ups - 20 seconds on / 20 seconds rest (3 times)

- Run in Place (RIP) 20 seconds on / 20 seconds rest (3 times

- Repeat for 3 rounds

Summary

1. Intermittent Fasting and High Intensity Interval Training are two tools that can be used to accelerate your results during your 14-Day Reboot. After the Reboot these tools may also be incorporated into your weekly routines to keep your body in balance.

What About Supplements?

What's On That X-ray?

I will never forget an infamous x-ray that changed the way I view supplements. We took an x-ray of a patient's lower back. In an x-ray of this type, along with the spine you can also see the bowels as well. When I looked at the x-ray, I couldn't believe what I saw. There were multiple solid ovals throughout this patient's bowel. I called in another doctor to look at the x-ray with me because I was confused! We then realized those ovals were supplements that had not digested. I asked the patient about her supplements. She informed us she was spending a lot of money on these supplements, and it came as quite a shock to her to find her body wasn't even absorbing them. As we looked closer and counted, we found there were two days of undigested and unabsorbed supplements in her digestive tract.

I share that because it opened my eyes to the truth about supplements—all supplements are not created equally. When you

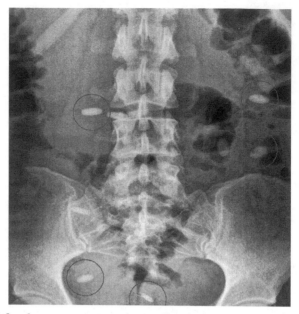

go in a natural foods store, you can immediately become overwhelmed with the many different types of the same supplements you find there. You can walk up and down the aisles and see a supplement for almost every part of your body. Many patients have come to me feeling overwhelmed and discouraged, not knowing what they should be taking or what is best for them.

Two Rules on Supplementation

When it comes to supplementation there are two rules I teach my patients. The first rule is to make sure it comes from a pure source. It's important to ask, "Does this have filler and preservatives that are going to prevent my body from even absorbing it?" The second rule is to stop guessing, and start testing. Let's break these down.

Quality

The quality of supplementation works a lot like the quality of alcohol. If I am going to buy some wine, typically I will see several brands of the same kind of wine separated between a top shelf, middle shelf and the bottom shelf. The higher priced and higher quality wines are on the top shelf, and the cheaper are on the bottom. It is the same with supplements. The lower you go, the cheaper it is, and the cheaper it is, the more impurities it has.

The following list of ingredients are ones typically used by lower quality companies. These are ingredients to stay away from and I would be wary of the companies using them.

1. Artificial Colorants. Various FD&C Blue, Green, Red, and Yellow are approved by the FDA. However, there is no reason that anyone needs to be consuming these substances, especially given the fact that some have been linked to ADHD and immune system problems.[1,2]

2. Titanium Dioxide. Titanium dioxide is often used as a colorant to give supplements and cosmetics a clean, white appearance. Studies have linked it to immune system problems, inflammation, DNA damage and kidney toxicity.[3]

3. BHT. Butylated Hydroxytoluene is a preservative used in a range of products (including petroleum, cosmetics and even embalming fluid) to improve the shelf-life of fat-based products. It is an antioxidant which prevents the breakdown of fats. BHT has been linked to liver toxicity and some forms of cancer.[4]

4. Magnesium Silicate. Magnesium Silicate is talc (as in talcum powder or baby powder) and it's used as an anti-caking agent in powder supplements. Studies have linked it to stomach cancer and lung inflammation.[5]

5. Sodium Benzoate. Consumers should be aware of anything containing benzene as it has been linked to various cancers. Sodium benzoate can form benzene if it's taken with ascorbic acid. Sodium benzoate has the potential to damage cells and DNA.[6]

6. Hydrogenated Oils. As discussed earlier in the book hydrogenated oils are man made and are damaging to our cells. There is no need to have added unhealthy fats to supplements which are supposed to be making you healthier.

You also want to check the expiration date on the supplement, especially if it is on sale. When supplements hit the shelf, they have already begun to degrade. If it is close to or past the expiration date, you do not want to put that in your body.

Another thing to check is its source—is it whole-food based or is it made in a lab? The further it is from how God created and intended it to be, the fewer benefits your body will derive from it.

Testing

For years in the nutritional world, if someone wanted a specific supplementation plan, he or she would go to see a nutritionist or a knowledgeable doctor in the field, and on the initial consultation they would go through the case history including any symptoms. The doctor/nutritionist would then recommend a supplement routine to help. It is like they were magicians and knew exactly what was happening internally without ever testing. To me that system, or train of thought, never made sense. You would never go to your medical doctor and say, "I think I have high cholesterol," and like magic the doctor would contemplate and say, "Yeah you are right, here is some medicine for that."

Chapter Eleven

The same process must take place for nutritional needs in the body. When it comes to supplementation we must test and not guess. There are many tests that can be ordered to determine exactly what you need, but unfortunately many of these tests are not run by your typical family practitioner. You would need to find a physician or nutritionist who has further specialties in functional medicine and/or holistic nutrition.

I often get asked "Why doesn't my doctor run these tests?" This is a great question. Here are a few reasons:

1. In many cases, insurance does not cover functional tests.

2. Most doctors are not trained to order functional tests. Let me explain:

Medical doctors are trained to run what I call "red-light testing". These test are used to determine if you have disease or not. This type of testing is good and has its place, but it can't be the only thing you are testing for.

Here is why I have a problem with this type of testing. Take for example, the total cholesterol test. While it does provide good information, it does not give us any details of how or why the particular condition is occurring. What is happening underneath the surface and within your body? What indications

What About Supplements?

do the tests give you of the internal workings and cellular metabolic activities which have caused you to have a finding of elevated cholesterol?

My preferred method of testing is to pose and answer functional questions like these:

- Are you able to metabolize and use the fats you are consuming?

- Are you able to metabolize glucose properly?

- Do you have the enzymes to properly break down the foods you are eating?

- How well is your liver detoxing your body?

- Are you deficient in amino acids, minerals, or vitamins?

- Do you have toxic build up in your system?

- How healthy is your microbiome (your gut health)?

Answering these questions allows us to peel back the onion and look at how the body is functioning underneath the surface, giving us the details necessary to prescribe the proper supplementation based on your specific

Chapter Eleven

needs. I call this "yellow-light testing." Yellow-light testing is a functional test which will determine if you are moving toward the green light of health or heading toward the red light of disease.

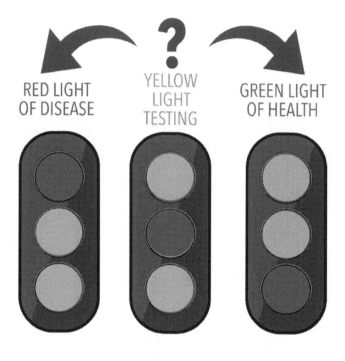

Whether you have a chronic condition or you are looking to optimize your health, visit our website, and click on the testing link to see my favorite and most comprehensive test for Nutritional Deficiencies.

What About Supplements?

Functional tests (yellow-light testing) are effective for patients experiencing:

- Mood disorders, including Depression and Anxiety

- Chronic Fatigue

- Digestive Complaints

- Chronic Pain

- Inflammatory Conditions

- Cardiovascular Risk

- Weight Issues/Dietary Guidance

- General Health

- Hormone Instability

- Sports Fitness Optimization

Now that we know to test and not to guess with supplementation, you

Chapter Eleven

may be asking "Why do you use recommend and use supplements in your 14-Day Reboot, without any testing?" I'll explain that next.

Long-Term vs. Short-Term

Let me first clarify what I mean by short-term and long-term supplementation. If someone was to twist his ankle, he doesn't need to get tested to see if he would benefit from a natural anti-inflammatory like curcumin. The evidence is clear that curcumin will help decrease inflammation and speed up the healing process. This would be short-term supplementation. Several reasons you would use short-term supplementation include:

- Cold/Flu

- Acute Injuries

- Specific Training Goals

- Boosting Immune System

- Traveling, especially air travel

Long-term supplementation is used when addressing specific body functions and chronic conditions, or for peak performance. These would be supplements that would, as the description implies, typically be taken for longer periods of time. Never guess and always test with long-term supplementation. During the 14-Day Reboot we recommend short-term supplementations to boost results and maximize healing.

Supplements for 14-Day Reboot

1. Body detox – When you want to detox the body, there are many options on the market, but what I look for is a product that has a two-step process. One step in the detox process is getting toxins out of the cells and supporting the liver to release these toxins into the digestive tract. Once the toxins are released into the bowels, then we need to prevent them from being reabsorbed by using something that will bind to them in the gut. This is where a second step is required. Activated charcoal is great to help bind toxins and release them through bowel movements.

2. Antioxidant/Anti-Inflammatory – As your body goes through the detox process, it will create free radicals, natural bi-products of the detoxification. Free radicals can attack your DNA. When this happens, it can speed up the aging process…and no one wants that! It is critical as you're detoxing, to get antioxidants that fight free radicals and lower inflammation.

Chapter Eleven

Herbs and supplementation, such as curcumin, are natural anti-oxidants and are anti-inflammatory.

3. Omega-3 Supplement – These help with rebuilding cellular membranes and having healthy cell membranes will facilitate the detox-ification process. Omega-3s also help fight inflammation, depression and anxiety, and promote brain and heart health. They need to be pure, however. Some are derived from bigger fish that carry a high toxic load. That is exactly what we are wanting to avoid, so, look for products sourced from smaller fish. I would also look for brands that purify the oils. Fish oil should never have a fishy aftertaste. This is a sign they may have gone rancid or are poor-quality products.

4. Proteins – Proteins are vital because they supply the necessary amino acids your body needs to rebuild. I recommend whey protein for its bioavailability and its sulfur compounds, which further aids in the detoxification process. Look for a whey protein that contains enzymes and probiotics, which help increase absorption, and it is a must for the whey to be sourced from grass-fed cows. If you choose a plant based protein, make sure it does not contain fillers.

What About Supplements?

There are a lot of things to consider when looking for high quality supplementation. I am constantly vetting suppliers, products, and health resources to make sure I am using the best quality products for my family and my patients.

Visit **the14dayrebootbook.com**
to check out my vetted resources.

I want to offer one final thought on supplementation. I mentioned above, when it comes to long-term supplementation always test, never guess. However, because of the lack of nutrients in our modern food supply, there are three supplements I believe are beneficial for most people. If you can't test and want to begin with something, I would start with what I call the "Core 3".

Core 3

1. Men's/Women's Multi-Vitamin – Vitamins and minerals are essential for normal cell function, growth and development. Since our bodies can't produce all the nutrients we need, and most times we can't get our daily recommended intake from food, I recommend a full-spectrum multivitamin that is specific to men or women.

Chapter Eleven

2. Vitamin D3 – Vitamin D is a critical nutrient for health and well-being. It supports healthy bones and teeth; promotes healthy skin; improves digestion; and supports immune system, brain, and nervous system health. It's also an important vitamin for women who are pregnant because a vitamin D deficiency may put the mother at greater risk of developing preeclampsia and needing a cesarean section delivery.

3. Balanced Omega – A balanced omega supplement supports cardiovascular health; reduces insulin resistance and inflammation; promotes healthy skin and hair; improves immune system function; and helps with cognitive health. A balanced omega supplement contains GLA, EPA/DHA, and ALA.

You can find information on my best nutritional supplement resources, personalized testing, and more at the14dayrebootbook.com.

The Reboot Lifestyle

Now it's time to get up and do something. Pack this book in your purse, bag, or car because we are going on the road. This section is filled with shopping lists, strategies and applicational information to help you head off to grocery store and make it happen. You will have all the information you need to know what to look for in your food and what to avoid. This section gives you the momentum to move past treating this like a new health fad and into creating a lifestyle that you will pass on to your friends, family, and most importantly, the next generation..

In this Section:

STARTING SOMETHING

NEW FOR YOUR

HEALTH ISN'T EASY,

BUT IT'S

ALWAYS WORTH IT.

12 Fad to Lifestyle

Hula hoops, pet rocks, yo-yo's, mood rings, Rubik's Cubes and lava lamps at one point many of these were "the thing". These and many other items are what would be considered fads. Yes, at some time in my life I had each one of those items. Just like at some point I have tried the South Beach Diet, the Ketogenic Diet, Whole 30, Nutrisystem, the Zone Diet, the Abs Diet, the Atkins Diet and probably a few others. The issue with many of them you can get short-term results (some in not so very healthy ways). But, although they are diets and systems that work well for short term results, people are rarely able to take these systems and make them a true lifestyle. Eventually the new feeling wears off and you start to lose interest, returning to your old lifestyle until the next hot trend. Starting something new for your health isn't easy, but it's always worth it. This book has given you many of the tools, strategies and principles to not only start your health journey, but to continue the journey and make it stick. In this chapter I outline how our family and hundreds of other families have made the switch and now live the Reboot Lifestyle.

The over arching anchor in my life is the belief that God has given each one of us a specific mission to accomplish. This belief always leads me to this question, "Are we doing our part to stay healthy enough to complete the mission?" Throughout our lives we will have many roles to play: mother, father, provider, friend, colleague and many others. Each one of these is critical and each one is of high importance. For me, one of my highest priorities is my family. With my family I always ask, am I passing down the habits and lifestyle that would give my kids and their kids the best opportunity for them to fulfill their God given potential, mission and assignments? This is why I am passionate about this book and more importantly, this chapter.

Yes, you can use the 14-Day Reboot to lose some weight, rebalance your hormones, and detox your body.
But if it ends there,
all I have created is just another fad diet.

That is the last thing I am looking to do. I want to create a lifestyle and not a fad. So how do we do that? How do we take all this "stuff" and create a true lifestyle? Let's dive in and see.

The Reboot Cycle

I love the changing of the seasons. Going from autumn to winter always brings back the memories of fun and family-filled holidays. Spring always triggers thoughts of freshness and new beginnings. Summer brings back the sights and sounds of playing outside until the sun goes down. I think you get picture. Our life revolves around the seasons. Each season brings change and I believe these are perfect opportunities to give yourself a refresh by pressing the reboot button.

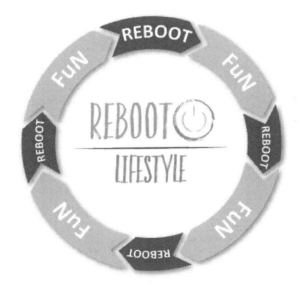

Chapter Twelve

Quarterly Reboots

While the FuN plan is how we should all be eating all the time, the reality is that we are not perfect and most of us may fall short at times. While vacation meals are part of the plan, even I begin to deviate and incorporate more vacations than I should at times. Yes, if my nutritional habits were my actual job, I could see myself getting fired and I teach this stuff! So, I really do know and understand this can be difficult, but this is also why my family and our reboot community do a planned 14-Day Reboot once a quarter. Four times a year, just like the seasons, we give our bodies a break and a time to get back on track. This is what a typical year looks like in my house. (Yes, we involve our kids. Go to www.the14dayrebootbook.com to download our Free E-Book on how to *End The Food Fight* with your kids.)

Let's start with the holidays – enough said. Coming off the holidays and with a new year on the horizon we always plug into our calendar our 14-Day Reboot and this is how we kick off the year (typically we start on the first Monday of the year). As you will see below, we then transition into our FuN plan and every three months we plug in another 14-Day Reboot. This cycle prevents our bodies from getting off balance hormonally. I mentioned before if it is your first time and you need more than 14 days to heal that's okay. But once you have reached your health goals this quarterly cycle helps you maintain your health change. Think of your body as a car you wouldn't wait until your engine broke down to then take it in for an oil change, that would be crazy. If you want your car to last and perform at its best, you need to have it regularly maintained. Your body is not much different, regular maintenance will keep you in tip top shape and functioning at an optimal level.

Here are a few of the benefits of the quarterly reboot cycle:

- No matter how good you eat, you will always come into contact with toxins which can, and will, build up in our bodies (bioaccumulation).

- Most of us start strong, but at some point (me included) we begin to veer of the path more than we should. Example: Holidays :)

- It helps prevent disease. It gives your body the breaks it needs through out the year to heal and repair.

- Each time you cycle through the reboot, your goal should be to learn something new and increase your commitment to healthy living.

- There is so much more than what is listed here!

Chapter Twelve

the14dayrebootbook.com will continue to grow with new content and information, so you can always plug back in and continue to learn and be re-inspired.

It's time to press the reboot button on your health.

Making it Easier, Not Harder

Shopping

One of my favorite programs is our "Shop with the Doc" workshop. I literally take patients to the supermarket and we shop together. They get to ask questions and learn how I shop for myself and my family (well how my wife shops for our family). When we shop I teach them the basics of shopping healthy and I show them what to look for. Basically, there are four questions you must always ask yourself when looking at an item (Hint-you learned these earlier):

4 Questions:

1. Does this food have any added sugars?

2. Does this food contain damaged fats or healthy fats?

3. Does this food contain toxic chemicals?

4. Does this food contain healthy or damaged proteins?

My wife, Jess, was at our local grocery store doing some shopping. Angela, a friend of the family, saw her and began to ask her questions about this "new diet" she just started. She picked up a few items from her cart and began to show my wife and she asked her if they would be good for her and also asked what she thought about the "new diet". Jess answered by saying, "I don't know much about all these diets, but I know that if I answer the simple questions of fats, proteins, sugar and toxins correctly, I will always be making a good choice for our family."

That is how simple it can be. If you just answer those four simple questions, then you never have to worry about diets and plans. Unfortunately, as they began going through some of the products in Angela's cart many of them did not pass the four question test. Many of the products had little to no "sugar" but they were filled with other additives, preservatives and chemical sweeteners. While this may have helped her lose some weight it would have been disastrous for her long-term health.

In our "Shop with the Doc" workshop, I also break down the basic concept of label reading. It is always important to make sure you are clear on what you are looking for when reading a label. This is where things can feel overwhelming, but I have a simple rule of thumb for you:

Never look at the top half of the label again.

What? Really? You mean don't count the calories, and check the fat content? No way. So why doesn't the top half matter?

Because if you get the bottom half right, the top half always takes care of itself.

What really matters is the ingredients that are inside. Always remember, the ingredients are listed from what occurs in the greatest quantity to what

Chapter Thirteen

occurs the least. So, whatever is written first, is what is present the most inside the item. Let's think back to our almonds and donuts example. It's about the effects the calories have on your hormones and not just the number of calories. Instead of looking for fat, carbs, protein and calorie content, focus on answering the four questions when looking at ingredients. That will be your simple test to guide you to make great hormone balancing, health increasing choices when it comes to your food choices.

Budgeting

Many people share with me how they just can't eat healthy because it costs too much. And yes, I understand eating healthy can add up and get expensive quickly, especially for those with growing families. We are a family of six. Trust me, I truly understand. But I have also tested it myself and seen that with a bit of creativity, budgeting and good planning anyone can begin making shifts to better food choices. Here is the budgeting concept I like to follow and share with others.

For simplification we are only looking at the three main macronutrients we need: fats, carbs, and proteins. Ideally, we would buy everything local, organic and as minimally processed as possible. But as I mentioned above that can get expensive quickly, so we start with the macronutrients which can have the most damaging effect on our body and that is proteins. If you remember back to the chapter on proteins not only do we need good healthy proteins to build a good healthy body, but proteins also have some of the highest levels of toxins which include hormones, antibiotics, pesticide build up, and other chemicals. Because of this, when patients are looking to begin the switch to healthier food products, I have them look at their budget and I tell them to spend money on buying the best quality proteins they can find and afford. Below is the order in which I would spend my budget:

Proteins First – Fats Second – Carbs Third

As you can see I would spend my money on proteins first, then fats and finally if the budget allowed for it, I would buy organic produce (fruits and veggies). This is where many people do the opposite. They think organic fruits and vegetables first, then they don't have enough money for the important foods our bodies need for rebuilding. This is why the proteins must be first.

Go to **the14dayrebootbook.com** and download our free *Good, Better, Best* PDF chart for the most common food items you will be purchasing.

Chapter Thirteen

On the PDF, you'll find options for most food categories and how to budget and prioritize grocery shopping. In each category you have worst, good, better and best options: In my family we try to stick with the better and best categories whenever possible. Rarely, if ever, do we buy from the worst category. (Unless we are talking about vacation meals, which we will discuss next, and even then we try to make less damaging choices.)

Even in the produce aisle you can budget even more by prioritizing what you should buy organic and what is safe to get as a non-organic option. There is a list that is updated yearly by the EWG (The Environmental Working Group) called, The Clean 15 and the Dirty Dozen. This list explains what fruit and veggies are being produced using the most pesticides and which ones are safer with less pesticides. The Dirty Dozen fruits and veggies would be on you "buy organic" list and other could be purchased conventionally to save money. This helps you budget while avoiding pesticides and toxins that can be present. As far as the Clean 15, these are the items you don't necessarily need to buy organic. Another good rule of thumb is if you peel it then it is safe enough to buy conventional, but if you don't peel it, organic is a better option. One more piece of information on label reading with organic products: organic does NOT mean it is GMO-free. Farmers can use GMO seeds then cultivate them organically. So be clear on that, if you want non-GMO products, it must be listed on the label.

Vacation Meals

What are vacation meals? Vacation meals are exactly what they sound like, it's a vacation, a mental break, a break from the norm. I learned this concept from my good friend and health leader, Dr. Ben Lerner. First, it's called a vacation meal, not a cheat meal. You are not cheating on your plan when it is part of your plan. Consider this: you would never work all year and not take a vacation. If you did, you would burn out and eventually quit or go insane. This is exactly what I see with most diet plans. Many people say something like "I'm starting this new plan and I'm never going back." Obviously, that is an unrealistic expectation and you are just setting yourself up for failure. Instead of setting up for failure, why not set yourself up for success by giving yourself the breaks necessary to keep you on plan. This is exactly why we include vacation meals in the FuN plan. By adding vacation meals to your plan, you have the mental breaks needed, and it allows you to still eat what you enjoy without the guilt of "cheating". I told you it was possible, "to have your cake and eat it too." The trick is these meals are planned, but just like time off from work, you need to get back to the FuN plan as scheduled. When you vacation from work you have a very specific time off and then you get right back to work. The same parameters apply here. Vacation meals are encouraged weekly, but these meals can't become the norm. If you stayed on a prolonged

Chapter Thirteen

vacation from work, you would be called…well…unemployed.

80/20 Food Rule

My 80/20 food rule is that 80% of my meals are on the FuN plan (these are minimally processed foods that answer the four basic food questions). And the other 20% of my meals are vacation meals (this is when I eat what I want, crave and desire). Let me show you what the math would look like:

7 Days/week x 3 Meals/day = 21 meals/week

21 meals per week x 20% = about 4 vacation meals/week

Since I intermittent fast a few days per week as I mentioned above, my number is actually three vacation meals/week. For three meals per week I eat what I want and I don't hold back; cheesecake yes, pizza yes, ice cream yes. I have reached the point that even on vacations I am looking for better options just because I enjoy them more and it makes me feel better.

Here are some options/tips on how to "vacation":

- Save the meals and do a full vacation day (this is great for Saturday or Sunday)

- Spread the meals out during the week.

- During your FuN plan if you are craving a non-approved meal/food, write it down and treat yourself when you have planned a vacation meal.

- Do some intermittent fasting the day after a vacation meal to minimize some of the effects.

Healthier vacation options:

Pizza: Instead of a chain restaurant, I look for somewhere that has fresh and local ingredients. For me a thinner and/or gluten free crust is a plus.

Burgers: McDonald's should never be an option. Every year, published articles report beef quality ratings for fast food restaurants. Choose a restaurant that uses an A or B rating. You can still feel good when you sink your teeth into that juicy burger. (And remember, burgers can be ordered in a lettuce wrap!)

Dessert: I look for homemade options at local restaurants. Typically, these have less additives and toxins. Nowadays health food stores have many great options with less toxic ingredients and less processed sugars.

Chapter Thirteen

Lateral Shifts

This is another tool to make things easier and not harder. Let's first consider "vertical shifts". A vertical shift is like going from eating pizza to eating broccoli, that is a hard sell and a very difficult change. Your kids would hate you. You would hate you. Lateral shifts are when you go from eating something you enjoy, to eating a healthier version. Lateral shifts are easy because all you are doing is changing the quality of the food. Here are some great examples:

Potato chips (pick your favorite)

Lateral Shift – Chips made with healthy coconut oil and no preservatives.

Pizza (pick your favorite)

Lateral Shift – Cauliflower Crust Pizza with cheese and toppings which are minimally processed.

Ice cream (pick your favorite)

Lateral Shift – Buying a home ice cream maker and make it with approved ingredients and sweeten with stevia and xylitol. Luckily, supermarkets are now carrying brands that follow these same parameters.

Making it Easier, Not Harder

For other lateral shifts, recipes, and more guidance visit: **the14dayrebootbook.com** and join our online family as we share tips, ideas, and encourage one another on our journey. This will give you the fuel to stay committed, engaged and to know that you can really do this!

Chapter Thirteen

Final Thoughts

I have given you a lot of information, a lot of tips and a lot of strategies to help you navigate the nutritional choices you will be making on a daily basis. Implementing these ideas beyond the 14-Day Reboot will help you go from just another fad to a real shift in your health and lifestyle.

In this section I outline a few final thoughts I have found helpful for those who want to go further faster, or for those of you who like the details. I will discuss macronutrients (proteins, carbs, and fats) and how much you should be eating of each. I will also discuss the benefits of having a trained professional help you set up a specific plan of attack for your personal needs and goals.

Macronutrients

What are macronutrients? It's real simple; they are the big three nutrients we need to consume on a daily basis. If you want more of a "book definition" of macronutrients, they are substances that are used for energy, growth, and bodily functions. In the human diet the three main sources of macronutrients(macros) are your fats, carbs and proteins. Our bodies cannot live without these three sources. We use them for energy, growth, healing, neurological function and blood circulation (basically for everything), but you already knew that from earlier.

Now that you know what to buy, the next question I usually get is, "How much of each macro should I be eating?" This is a great question and I purposely did not answer it previously. It has been my experience that the simpler we keep things, the better it is. Just by making the switches mentioned in this book, it will be enough for most people to see some amazing changes. My typical answer on how much you should eat is that you should eat until you are satisfied (you shouldn't feel overly stuffed).

I will give you specific ranges for the Reboot and FuN plans, but I am weary of doing so because it varies for everyone. Your personal macronutrient profile will be greatly determined by activity level, gender, age and many other factors. To truly have a personalized profile I would suggest a one-on-one consultation with one of our trained health coaches.

Final Thoughts

Here are the general macro numbers for both plans:

	Proteins	Fats	Carbs
Reboot Plan	15-25%	55-65%	8-10%
FuN Plan	15-25%	65-75%	15-25%

Calculating Macro's

Earlier in the book I mentioned you should not to be concerned with calories and while this is true, in order to calculate your personal macronutrient profile you will need to know how many calories you are consuming of each macro.

Here is a chart based on a 2,000 calorie diet to reference when meal planning. Remember these calculations will vary depending on many factors.

	Carbs	Fats	Protein
REBOOT %	8–10%	65–75%	15–25%
REBOOT grams	40-50-g	145-165-g	75-125g
FuN %	15-25%	55-65%	15-25%
FuN grams	75-125g	125-145g	75-125g

Chapter Fourteen

A note on calculating "Net Carbs": when reading labels, look at the carbs and subtract "total fiber" from "total carbs".

Carbs in the form of fiber are indigestible and help stabilize your insulin. This aids in detoxification and helps with bowel motility.

Example: 1 Cup of Blackberries has about
15 grams of Carbs and 8 grams of Fiber
15 grams Carbs
- 8 grams Fiber
= 7 grams Net Carbs

WOW!!! This is why berries are super foods; high in antioxidants and fiber while low in sugar (and they taste great too)!

We have made this easy for you and included a bonus carb counter PDF with the most common carbs and the net carbs per servings at the14dayrebootbook.com

When to begin focusing on macros with our plans:

- When you have hit a plateau with your health goals

- Once you are comfortable and fully understand both Reboot and
  FuN plans

- You want to go further faster and want the best results

- If you are the type of person who needs the details to stay on track

- You know your health is vitally important, and you are ready to do
  whatever it takes to regain it

In all of these cases, I would suggest a one-on-one consultation with
one of our trained coaches to help you set up your personalized plan.

Coaching

Growing up watching and loving sports, I have seen the benefit of good
coaching. A coach is someone who can help set a plan that is specific to you
and will give you the best results. A great coach also brings out the best in
you through accountability, support and encouragement. Coaches keep you on
track and keep you moving towards your goal. Most people believe coaching
is expensive and unaffordable. I have personally trained a group of coaches
and have set up affordable plans to set up macronutrient profiles, goals and
ongoing accountability if necessary.

Chapter Fourteen

Final Thoughts…The End (or maybe just the beginning?)

Fast forward…as I sit hear thinking about the past twenty-five plus years, since that awful day with the tie around my neck. I can't help but to think about my grandfather who passed away when I was eighteen. As if it was yesterday, I remember being in the garage organizing, while my grandfather was in the house watching tv. My next memory is of the confusion I experience when I saw an ambulance pull up to my house and take him to the hospital. Within a month he passed from kidney and liver failure. Both of my grandmothers suffered for last sixteen years of their lives. One was bed ridden for more than twelve years with Alzheimer's, the other was in and out of the hospital constantly and due to her extensive list of health conditions lived on eighteen medications to be able to "function". Here is the problem in all of these cases they did what the doctors told them to do which was to eat less fat, walk and take medications to keep them "well". And while some might argue it must be genetic, well their parents all lived to be one-hundred plus with vibrant health until the last few years. Hmm..genetics?

Genes are like light switches; you can turn them on and off by the lifestyle choices you make. I was told early on that my health issues were "in my genes". I was told early on that my health issues were "in my genes". Now with kids of my own and thinking of my family history and my own story, I am so thankful for all that has transpired in my life. When it comes to my nutrition, I am not perfect, but I am progressing. I'm not where I want to be, but I am not where I used to be. Empowered with the tools in this book I can confidently know that I am passing down a lifestyle to my kids that will lead them down a better path, a path which will allow them to experience a better expression of who they are meant to be. This is not the end, it is just the beginning of a new lifestyle you get to pass on to future generations.

Chapter Fourteen

Reboot Plan & Daily Guide

15

The goal is to shift your mindset to a new way of thinking—no more fads or trends. This time, the efforts you make will turn into habits and will change your life forever.

THE REBOOT PLAN

This is a short term 14-day plan specially designed to reduce inflammation, restore cell membrane function, aid in detoxification, regulate hormones, and eliminate sugar cravings. It is geared towards weight loss and promotes the use of fat as your primary fuel source.

The REBOOT Plan can be used in two ways:

FIRST: to heal the body from years of accumulated damage Use until you reach your desired goals.

SECOND: on a cyclical basis to REBOOT and rebalance our bodies. We recommend this plan be used once a quarter (4x/year) for 14 days.

WE'VE MADE THIS SIMPLE

1. Pick your **PROTOCOL**

2. Follow **THREE RULES** of the 14-Day Reboot

3. **MAXIMIZE** your Results with our Reboot Supplements at **the14dayrebootbook.com**

1. Pick Your Protocol

[ ] Beginner

[ ] Intermediate

[ ] Advanced Reboot

If this is your first 14-Day Reboot, you may want to start at the Beginner Level. Please read through each plan to see which one seems the most achievable right now.

A. BEGINNER REBOOT

BREAKFAST: Protein shake (see Appendix)

LUNCH & DINNER: A REBOOT approved meal

You can always replace any meal with a shake.

IMPORTANT: Drink more water than you would normally drink – even if you do not feel thirsty.

In the Intermediate and Advanced REBOOT, intermittent fasting (IF) in the morning is necessary to help accelerate your results. See IF instructions.

B. INTERMEDIATE REBOOT

Skip Breakfast

Enjoy a REBOOT Approved Lunch and Dinner or opt for a protein shake for Lunch

C. ADVANCED REBOOT

Day 1 - Fast from dinner to dinner (24 hours).

If you can, fast until breakfast (36 hours).

Drink plenty of water.

Days 2–14 - Use the Intermediate plan, but also eliminate dairy.

2. Follow Three Rules

RULE ONE: Remove all Grains, Sugars & Sugary Fruits. Make a lateral shift to REBOOT approved carbs, flours & produce.

RULE TWO: Remove all Unhealthy Fats. Make a lateral shift to good healthy fats.

RULE THREE: Remove all Damaged Proteins. Make a lateral shift to REBOOT approved proteins. Excess protein turns to sugar. Moderate your consumption.

14-Day Meal Plan + Daily Guide

These recipes are a suggestion only. You may eat any food combination that is in the approved REBOOT food list. Many of these meals are great to multiply or re-purpose. Several meals are marked as ROUND TWO indicated by this symbol **[R2]**. Those feature leftovers that may be used in a second meal. Round Two meals are time savers because you cook once, and enjoy twice (or more). Use this meal plan exactly as written out, or mix it up as you please.

The recipes for your meal plan are online at: **the14dayrebootbook.com** listed under the REBOOT APPROVED blog category.

Chapter Fifteen

Day 1 - Meal Plan

	Breakfast	Lunch	Dinner
Basic REBOOT	Protein Shake	Whey Protein Shake or a REBOOT Approved Meal	**RECIPE:** Grilled Chicken with Squash & Onions
Advanced REBOOT	Intermittent Fast No breakfast, take supplements with Lunch	**RECIPE:** Garden Salad with Fresh Caught Canned Tuna Olive oil & Lemon Wedge	No eating or snacking after dinner
Supplement Plan	Upon waking, 2 Cell Detox with water. Wait 30 minutes for breakfast.	Meal Time: 2 Daily Defense & 2 Optimal Omega	Before Bed - 2 Body Detox with water a minimum of 1 hour after dinner

Day 2 - Meal Plan

	Breakfast	Lunch	Dinner
Basic REBOOT	Protein Shake	Whey Protein Shake or a REBOOT Approved Meal	**RECIPE:** Salmon with Olive Oil & Lemon - Roasted Broccoli
Advanced REBOOT	Intermittent Fast No breakfast, take supplements with Lunch	**RECIPE:** Cauliflower Soup & Small Garden Salad	No eating or snacking after dinner
Supplement Plan	Upon waking, 2 Cell Detox with water. Wait 30 minutes for breakfast.	Meal Time: 2 Daily Defense & 2 Optimal Omega	Before Bed - 2 Body Detox with water a minimum of 1 hour after dinner

FOCUS

The beginning of a cleansing protocol can be challenging. You are helping your body begin to release toxins that have been stored for an extended period of time. This cleanse will focus on your major detoxification organs; liver, kidneys, and colon.

You Might Experience:

Fatigue	Headaches	Hunger
Thirst	Irritability	Changes in mood

JOURNAL about your excitement. Write down your feelings about this journey.

_____

_____

_____

_____

_____

_____

_____

_____

_____

_____

Day 3 - Meal Plan

	Breakfast	Lunch	Dinner
Basic REBOOT	Protein Shake	Whey Protein Shake or a REBOOT Approved Meal	RECIPE: Steak with Brussels Sprouts & Kale
Advanced REBOOT	Intermittent Fast No breakfast, take supplements with Lunch	RECIPE: Chicken Lettuce Wraps & Cauliflower Soup [R2]	No eating or snacking after dinner
Supplement Plan	Upon waking, 4 Cell Detox with water. Wait 30 minutes for breakfast.	Meal Time: 2 Daily Defense & 2 Optimal Omega	Before Bed - 4 Body Detox with water a minimum of 1 hour after dinner

Day 4 - Meal Plan

	Breakfast	Lunch	Dinner
Basic REBOOT	Protein Shake	Whey Protein Shake or a REBOOT Approved Meal	RECIPE: Coconut Curry Chicken with Cucumber Salad
Advanced REBOOT	Intermittent Fast No breakfast, take supplements with Lunch	RECIPE: Hard Boiled Egg mixed with Olive Oil on Garden Salad	No eating or snacking after dinner
Supplement Plan	Upon waking, 4 Cell Detox with water. Wait 30 minutes for breakfast.	Meal Time: 2 Daily Defense & 2 Optimal Omega	Before Bed - 4 Body Detox with water a minimum of 1 hour after dinner

FOCUS

You're beginning to increase the amount of toxins you're releasing. You've started burning fat by changing the way you eat. You're mobilizing those toxins and eliminating them by taking your supplements daily.

You Might Experience:

Previous symptoms plus
Skin rashes or irritation

Changes in mood
Flu like symptoms

JOURNAL - List any changes you've made to this guide to customize it to your style?

_____

_____

_____

_____

_____

_____

_____

_____

_____

Day 5 - Meal Plan

	Breakfast	Lunch	Dinner
Basic REBOOT	Protein Shake	Whey Protein Shake or a REBOOT Approved Meal	**RECIPE:** Asparagus Omelet
Advanced REBOOT	Intermittent Fast No breakfast, take supplements with Lunch	**RECIPE:** Coconut Curry Chicken [R2]	No eating or snacking after dinner
Supplement Plan	Upon waking, 4 Cell Detox with water. Wait 30 minutes for breakfast.	Meal Time: 2 Daily Defense & 2 Optimal Omega	Before Bed - 4 Body Detox with water a minimum of 1 hour after dinner

Day 6 - Meal Plan

	Breakfast	Lunch	Dinner
Basic REBOOT	Protein Shake	Whey Protein Shake or a REBOOT Approved Meal	**RECIPE:** Roast Turkey & Green Beans
Advanced REBOOT	Intermittent Fast No breakfast, take supplements with Lunch	**RECIPE:** Sweet & Savory Salad	No eating or snacking after dinner
Supplement Plan	Upon waking, 4 Cell Detox with water. Wait 30 minutes for breakfast.	Meal Time: 2 Daily Defense & 2 Optimal Omega	Before Bed - 4 Body Detox with water a minimum of 1 hour after dinner

FOCUS

Did you know that fat is where our body stores toxins? Your cleanse is helping you breakdown fat and finally rid your body of toxins.

JOURNAL - What is your greatest struggle with this plan right now?

_____

_____

_____

_____

_____

_____

_____

_____

_____

_____

_____

_____

_____

Day 7 - Meal Plan

	Breakfast	Lunch	Dinner
Basic REBOOT	Protein Shake	Whey Protein Shake or a REBOOT Approved Meal	**RECIPE:** Red Curry Chicken with Broccoli
Advanced REBOOT	Intermittent Fast No breakfast, take supplements with Lunch	**RECIPE:** Italian Sausage Soup	No eating or snacking after dinner
Supplement Plan	Upon waking, 3 Cell Detox with water. Wait 30 minutes for breakfast.	3 Cell Detox with water (before or after lunch) Meal Time: 2 Daily Defense & 2 Optimal Omega	Before Bed - 6 Body Detox with water a minimum of 1 hour after dinner

Day 8 - Meal Plan

	Breakfast	Lunch	Dinner
Basic REBOOT	Protein Shake	Whey Protein Shake or a REBOOT Approved Meal	**RECIPE:** Huevos Ranchero Frittata
Advanced REBOOT	Intermittent Fast No breakfast, take supplements with Lunch	**RECIPE:** Sweet Turkey Salad [R2]	No eating or snacking after dinner
Supplement Plan	Upon waking, 3 Cell Detox with water. Wait 30 minutes for breakfast.	3 Cell Detox with water (before or after lunch) Meal Time: 2 Daily Defense & 2 Optimal Omega	Before Bed - 6 Body Detox with water a minimum of 1 hour after dinner

FOCUS

Days 7-10 can be the most challenging, you're hitting the peak of your REBOOT. The supplements combined with your diet are supporting the mobilization and elimination of toxins.

JOURNAL - What part your favorite part about this plan so far?

You Might Experience:
Increased bowel movements and urination
(if bowl movements have decreased, take magnesium to help elimination)

_____

_____

_____

_____

_____

_____

_____

_____

_____

_____

Day 9 - Meal Plan

	Breakfast	Lunch	Dinner
Basic REBOOT	Protein Shake	Whey Protein Shake or a REBOOT Approved Meal	**RECIPE:** Blueberry Pancakes & Chicken Sausage
Advanced REBOOT	Intermittent Fast No breakfast, take supplements with Lunch	**RECIPE:** Red Curry Chicken [R2]	No eating or snacking after dinner
Supplement Plan	Upon waking, 3 Cell Detox with water. Wait 30 minutes for breakfast.	3 Cell Detox with water (before or after lunch) Meal Time: 2 Daily Defense & 2 Optimal Omega	Before Bed - 6 Body Detox with water a minimum of 1 hour after dinner

Day 10 - Meal Plan

	Breakfast	Lunch	Dinner
Basic REBOOT	Protein Shake	Whey Protein Shake or a REBOOT Approved Meal	**RECIPE:** Shredded Beef with Jicama Salad
Advanced REBOOT	Intermittent Fast No breakfast, take supplements with Lunch	**RECIPE:** Italian Sausage Soup [R2]	No eating or snacking after dinner
Supplement Plan	Upon waking, 3 Cell Detox with water. Wait 30 minutes for breakfast.	3 Cell Detox with water (before or after lunch) Meal Time: 2 Daily Defense & 2 Optimal Omega	Before Bed - 6 Body Detox with water a minimum of 1 hour after dinner

FOCUS

JOURNAL - List the benefits of this plan that you're experiencing.

_____

_____

_____

_____

_____

_____

_____

_____

_____

_____

_____

_____

_____

_____

Day 11 - Meal Plan

	Breakfast	Lunch	Dinner
Basic REBOOT	Protein Shake	Whey Protein Shake or a REBOOT Approved Meal	**RECIPE:** Swedish Meatballs Over Mashed Cauliflower
Advanced REBOOT	Intermittent Fast No breakfast, take supplements with Lunch	**RECIPE:** Hard Boiled Egg, 1/2 apple, Olives, Cucumber, Nuts	No eating or snacking after dinner
Supplement Plan	Upon waking, 4 Cell Detox with water. Wait 30 minutes for breakfast.	Meal Time: 2 Daily Defense & 2 Optimal Omega	Before Bed - 4 Body Detox with water a minimum of 1 hour after dinner

Day 12 - Meal Plan

	Breakfast	Lunch	Dinner
Basic REBOOT	Protein Shake	Whey Protein Shake or a REBOOT Approved Meal	**RECIPE:** Shredded Beef with Jicama Salad
Advanced REBOOT	Intermittent Fast No breakfast, take supplements with Lunch	**RECIPE:** Italian Sausage Soup [R2]	No eating or snacking after dinner
Supplement Plan	Upon waking, 4 Cell Detox with water. Wait 30 minutes for breakfast.	Meal Time: 2 Daily Defense & 2 Optimal Omega	Before Bed - 4 Body Detox with water a minimum of 1 hour after dinner

FOCUS

You should be starting to notice the benefits of your REBOOT. If you've changed your diet, you'll notice that food is starting to taste better. At first, your new diet might have seemed bland, but now you're getting used to these new flavors.

JOURNAL - What have you changed in this plan to customize it to your style?

> **You Might Experience:**
> Improved energy   Weight loss
> Improved sleep   Improved digestion

_____

_____

_____

_____

_____

_____

_____

_____

_____

Day 13 - Meal Plan

	Breakfast	Lunch	Dinner
Basic REBOOT	Protein Shake	Whey Protein Shake or a REBOOT Approved Meal	**RECIPE:** Fish Tacos with Cauliflower Rice [R2]
Advanced REBOOT	Intermittent Fast No breakfast, take supplements with Lunch	**RECIPE:** Meatball Vegetable Soup [R2]	No eating or snacking after dinner
Supplement Plan	Upon waking, 2 Cell Detox with water. Wait 30 minutes for breakfast.	Meal Time: 2 Daily Defense & 2 Optimal Omega	Before Bed - 2 Body Detox with water a minimum of 1 hour after dinner

Day 14 - Meal Plan

	Breakfast	Lunch	Dinner
Basic REBOOT	Protein Shake	Whey Protein Shake or a REBOOT Approved Meal	**RECIPE:** Ginger Beef with Snap Peas
Advanced REBOOT	Intermittent Fast No breakfast, take supplements with Lunch	**RECIPE:** Taco Lettuce Boats	No eating or snacking after dinner
Supplement Plan	Upon waking, 2 Cell Detox with water. Wait 30 minutes for breakfast.	Meal Time: 2 Daily Defense & 2 Optimal Omega	Before Bed - 2 Body Detox with water a minimum of 1 hour after dinner

FOCUS

You did it! A few more days and you are done. Congrats! Focus on how you feel and journal about the amazing changes you have experienced.

JOURNAL - CONGRATULATIONS! Write your thoughts about this journey.

_____

You Might Experience:
Improved energy   Weight loss
Improved sleep   Improved digestion
            And overall feeling of well being

_____

_____

_____

_____

_____

_____

_____

_____

Appendix - Food Lists & References

This section is loaded with lists, charts and guides to help you along the 14-Day Reboot path. Refer to these lists when grocery shopping, snacking, and meal planning.

> "ONCE YOU KNOW HOW TO FEED YOUR BODY CORRECTLY, YOUR BODY WILL BE BETTER EQUIPPED TO CORRECT ITSELF."

Reboot & FuN Produce List

High-fiber, low-sugar carbohydrate produce.
Best carbohydrate choice. Consume any time of day

VEGETABLES

Arugula
Asparagus
Avocado
Bamboo Shoots
Bean Sprouts
Bell Peppers
Broad Beans
Broccoli
Brussel Sprouts
Cabbage
Cauliflower
Celery
Collard Greens
Cucumber
Eggplant
Endive
Fennel
Garlic
Ginger Root
Green Beans
Hearts of Palm
Herbs
Jicama
Jalepeno Pepper
Kale
Kohlrabi
Lettuces

Mushrooms
Mustard Greens
Olives
Onions
Radish
Radicchio
Snap Beans
Snow Peas
Shallots
Spinach
Spaghetti Squash
Summer Squash
Swiss Chard
Tomato
Turnip Greens
Watercress
Zucchini

FRUIT

Blackberries
Blueberries
Boysenberries
Elderberries
Gooseberries
Granny Smith Apples
Lemon/Lime
Raspberries
Strawberries

FuN Produce List

Not for Reboot plan. Eat in moderation.
Moderate-fiber, moderate-glycemic carbohydrates

Artichokes
Barley
Brown Rice
Buckwheat
Bulgar
Rye
Steel Cut Oats
Leeks
Legumes
Lima Beans
Black Beans
Chick Peas
Kidney Beans
Great Northern
Cannelini
Navy Beans
Pinto Beans
Split Peas
White or Yellow Beans
Okra
Pumpkin

Squash
Sweet Potato
Turnip
Fruit
Apples
Apricots
Cherries
Grapefruit
Kiwi
Melon
Nectaries
Oranges
Passion Fruit
Peaches
Pears
Persimmons
Plums
Pomegranate
Prunes
Tangerines

Appendix

FuN Produce List

VEGETABLES, TUBERS & GRAINS

Banana
Beet
Carrot
Corn
Dates
Grapes
Honey
Watermelon
Mango
Papaya
Potatoes

Healthy Fats List

Low-to-no processing. Raw. Organic.
Approved for FuN & REBOOT Plans

	Raw for Eating	Butters/Oils	Milk	Flour
ALMOND	X	Butter & Oil	X	X
AVOCADO	X	Low heat		
CASHEWS	X	Do not heat	X	
CHIA SEED	X	---	---	---
COCONUT	X	Butter & Oil For high heat	X	X
COD LIVER	X	Do not heat	---	------
GRAPE SEED	X	Medium heat	---	---
FLAXSEED	X	Do not heat	---	X
HEMP SEED	X	Do not heat	---	---
MACADAMIA	X	Butter	---	---
OLIVE	X	For low heat	---	---
PECANS	X	---	---	---
PINE NUTS	X	---	---	------
PUMPKIN SEEDS	X	Butter	---	---
SESAME SEEDS	X	Raw Tahini	---	---
WALNUTS	X	Do not heat	---	---
RAW BUTTER	X			

Appendix

Proteins
You Are What Your Food Ate

Your budget may determine the quality of proteins you are able to eat. The chart below ranks different protein sources beginning with things you should avoid if at all possible and moving up to the best possible sources. This chart covers the major animal proteins, it does not address every possible animal protein, but the principles can be applied other meats.

AVOID	GOOD	BETTER	BEST
Conventional Factory Farmed Poultry	Organic, Hormone Free Poultry	Organic Free Range Poultry	Local Organic Pasture Raised Poultry
Grain-Fed Beef or Pork, All processed meats	Organic Beef or Pork	Organic Grass Fed Beef	Local Organic 100% Grass Fed and Finished Beef, No Pork
Farm Raised Large Fish, Fish Prone to Toxins, Imitation Seafood, Shellfish	Farm Raised Fish with Low Toxic Load	Wild Caught Fish	Wild Caught Fish with Low Toxic Load and High Omega 3's, No Shellfish

CHOOSING PROTEIN	CHOOSING FATS	CHOOSING PRODUCE
Select protein that is: Organic Grass Fed Raised in a natural environment And fed a natural diet	Increase healthy fats: Organic, Non-GMO, Unrefined Extra Virgin Coconut Avocado, Walnut, Flaxseed, Extra Virgin Olive	See the list on the next page for our produce suggestions
Nuts & Seeds Should be organic & raw		Organic vs. Conventional

Purchase Health
MASTER OF LABELS

Be mindful when making the lateral shift products that contain no added sugar, because they replace many of the sugars with chemicals and other additives which are toxic to our cells and a detriment to our health.

STOP BUYING

- Monosodium Glutamate (MSG)

- Hydrolyzed or Autolyzed products

- Artificial sweeteners - sucralose/Splenda, aspartame/Nutrasweet, Equal, fructose, glucose, dextrose, sucrose

- Hydrogenated or partially hydrogenated products - oils: canola, vegetable, corn, soybean, safflower, sunflower, cottonseed

- Refined flour - white flour, whole wheat flour, corn starch, corn meal

- Additives, Colorings, Preservatives

- GMO produce

START

- Looking for minimal ingredients (less the better)

- Looking for natural ingredients (words you can pronounce and identify outside a laboratory)

- Buying more foods without labels (i.e. fruits and vegetables)

- Reading every label on every single thing you buy

- Putting items back on the shelf if they contain unnatural or toxic ingredients (if it doesn't come from the ground or grow in a tree)

- Looking for non-GMO products & produce

Produce
Organic vs. Conventional

It's best to always buy organic. However, it can get very expensive. Follow this guide to help save on money and make the best choice for your body.

Select Organic	Conventional OK
Bell Peppers	Asparagus
Celery	Avocado
Granny Smith Apples	Cabbage
Spinach	Cauliflower
All berries	Grapefruit
	Eggplant
	Onions

The produce not mentioned above can be purchased either organic or conventional. Obviously, organic is the best choice for your body.

Sweeteners
Whole Food Sugars

Sugar can be homemade with these organic ingredients. They are approved on the FuN Plan, but not to be consumed while Rebooting.

Apple Sauce
Fruit Juice
Banana Puree
Whole Dried Fruits

Plant-Based, Safer Sugars

Sugar can be homemade with these organic ingredients.

Stevia
Lakanto
Sugar Alcohols
Chicory Root
Xylitol

Protein Shakes

Protein shakes are simples alternatives, take minimal time to prepare, and taste delicious! Here's the process:

Pick a base: coconut milk, almond milk, unsweetened yogurt, or water

Add protein: high quality whey or plant-based

Pick add-ins: avocado, chia seeds, cacao powder, frozen fruit, ice cubes, cinnamon (so many options!)

Blend it up and enjoy!

Snack Ideas

Snacking is permitted between meals only if you're hungry.
Snacks are open to all raw items on your food list.

Examples:
1/4 cup Berries
2 Tbls Nut Butter
Cucumber Wheels
Guacamole
Celery
1/2 Avocado
Granny Smith Apple
1/4 c Nuts & Seeds
Almond Power Bar
Smoothie
Walnuts, Pecans or Almonds
Broccoli & Cauliflower
Zucchini Spears
Red Pepper Slices

REFERENCES

CHAPTER THREE

1. Brenda Davis, RD. (2008, August) - Defeating Diabetes: Lessons From the Marshall Islands, - Today's Dietitian, Vol. 10 No. 8 P. 24

2. https://www.mottchildren.org/health-library/sig49202 - Author: Healthwise Staff - Medical Review: William H. Blahd, Jr., MD, FACEP - Emergency Medicine & Adam Husney, MD - Family Medicine & Kathleen Romito, MD - Family Medicine & H. Michael O'Connor, MD, MMEd, FRCPC - Emergency Medicine & Martin J. Gabica, MD - Family Medicine (September 23, 2018). How a scrape heals.

3. https://kidshealth.org/en/teens/colds.html – Patricia Solo-Josephson, MD. (2017, June). Coping With Colds.

CHAPTER SEVEN

1. Effects of toxins - https://naturemed.org/how-toxins-cause-disease/ Author – Dr. Joseph Pizzorno, 2017

2. https://monographs.iarc.fr/wp-content/uploads/2018/06/mono101-005.pdf - International Agency for Research on Cancer, Review 2012

3. Material Safety Data Sheet (MSDS)

4. Journal of the American College of Toxicology; Vol. 2, No 7, 1983

5. Tap water - https://www.ewg.org/news/news-releases/2009/12/09/press-release-updated-tap-water-databases-and-drinking-water-quality - Environmental Working Group, 2009

CHAPTER EIGHT

1. http://www.espn.com/nfl/story/_/id/15454487/nfl-warns-eating-too-much-meat-mexico-china-result-positive-test

2. https://www.helladelicious.com/blog/2011/08/diet-and-culture-of-abkhasian-centenarians/

3. https://www.westonaprice.org/health-topics/in-his-footsteps/diet-of-mongolia/

CHAPTER NINE

1. SAD - https://draxe.com/charts-american-diet/

CHAPTER TEN

IF:

1. https://www.ncbi.nim.nih.gov/pubmed/277376774
2. https://www.ncbi.nim.nih.gov/pmc/articles/pmc5394735/
3. https://www.ncbi.nim.nih.gov/pubmed/23112824/
4. https://www.ncbi.nim.nih.gov/pmc/articles/pmc4549297
5. https://www.ncbi.nim.nih.gov/pubmed/23755298
6. https://www.ncbi.nim.nih.gov/pmc/articles/pmc3956913/

HIIT:

1. https://www.ncbi.nlm.nih.gov/pubmed/25675374
2. https://www.ncbi.nlm.nih.gov/pmc/articles/PMC2991639/

CHAPTER ELEVEN

1. https://www.fda.gov/food/ingredientspackaginglabeling/foodadditivesingredients/ucm094211.htm#types
2. https://search.proquest.com/openview/a8023da8e9b4d6ca335858dcdcd889f0/1?pq-origsite=g-scholar&cbl=32528
3. https://www.ncbi.nlm.nih.gov/pubmed/24631018
4. https://www.researchgate.net/profile/AbdelMajeed_Safer/publication/13085157_Hepatotoxic-ity_induced_by_the_anti-oxidant_food_additive_butylated_hydroxytoluene_BHT_in_rats_An_electron_microscopical_study/links/58cfabfb92851c5009ef98dc/Hepatotoxicit
5. https://www.jstage.jst.go.jp/article/indhealth/advpub/0/advpub_2013-0105/_article
6. https://www.ncbi.nlm.nih.gov/pubmed/21130826

Appendix

Made in the USA
Columbia, SC
16 May 2021